THE GHERANDA SANHITA,

A TREATISE ON

HATHA YOGA

D1880579

THE GHERANDA SANHITA,

A TREATISE ON

HATHA YOGA,

TRANSLATED
FROM THE ORIGINAL SANSKRIT,

by

SRIS CHANDRA VASU,

B. A., F. T. S.,

TRANSLATOR OF 'SHIVA SANHITA,' 'PANINI,' &C.

PUBLISHED FOR THE BOMBAY THEOSOPHICAL
PUBLICATION FUND

by

TOOKARAM TATYA, F. T. S.

GYAN

Published by

Gyan Publishing House
5, Ansari Road
Daryaganj, New Delhi-110002
Phone: 011-47034999, 9811692060
E-mail: books@gyanbooks.com

Distribution Network
gyanbooks.com
India, USA, Canada, UK, Australia, France

© Publisher

All rights reserved. No part of this work may be reproduced, stored, adapted, or transmitted in any form or by any means, electronic, mechanical, photocopying, micro-filming, recording or otherwise, or translated in any language, without the prior written permission of the copyright owner and the publisher.

ISBN : 978-81-212-6154-8 (PB)
First Published, 1895

2nd Impression 2021

Printed at: Gyan Press, Delhi.

The book is sold subject to the condition that it shall not, by way of trade or otherwise, be lent, resold, hired out, or otherwise circulated without the prior publisher's written consent.

The Gheranda Sanhita, A treatise on Hatha Yoga
Author: Sris Chandra Vasu

THE GHERAṆḌA SANHITA,

A TREATISE ON

HATHA YOGA,

TRANSLATED

FROM THE ORIGINAL SANSKRIT,

BY

SRIS CHANDRA VASU, B. A., F. T. S.,

TRANSLATOR OF 'SHIVA SANHITÂ,' 'PÂNINI,' &c.

PUBLISHED FOR THE BOMBAY THEOSOPHICAL PUBLICATION FUND

BY

TOOKARAM TATYA, F. T. S.

1895.

HARIDAS.

हरिदास.

TO

SHRI GURU DEVA,

WHOSE

PRACTICAL ILLUSTRATIONS AND TEACHINGS
CONVINCED THE TRANSLATOR, OF THE
REALITY, UTILITY, AND THE
IMMENSE ADVANTAGES
OF

HATHA YOGA,

THIS TRANSLATION IS RESPECTFULLY

DEDICATED

BY

HIS HUMBLE SEVAKA,

THE TRANSLATOR.

THE
GHERAṆḌA SANHITA

SALUTATION.

I salute that Âdîśvara (The First Lord) who taught first the. science of Hatha Yoga. This is a ladder for climbing ṭo the higher heights of Râja Yoga.

CONTENTS.

FIRST LESSON.

SECOND LESSON.

THIRD LESSON.

FOURTH LESSON.

FIFTH LESSON.

SIXTH LESSON.

SEVENTH LESSON.

APPENDIX.

It was in the year 1839 that I had returned to Lahore, after having visited the European continent and my native country. I enjoyed the pleasure, on my return, of being the companion of General Ventura, who was also hastening to India to resume his duties. On our voyage, we had many conversations, among which, the events which had happened during my absence from Lahore underwent discussion. On that occasion, the General related to me an occurrence which, at first, I could scarcely believe, thinking it a pure invention or a mere joke; but I soon became persuaded that he was in earnest. I give it here with the remark only, that, after having arrived at Lahore, I heard it confirmed by other persons, in whose statements I could also place confidence.

Runjeet Sing—thus runs the narrative—was told that a saat, or faqueer, living in the mountains, was able to keep himself in a state resembling death, and would allow himself to be even buried, without injuring or endangering his life, provided they would remove or release him from the grave after expiration of a fixed time, he being in the possession of the means of resuscitating himself again. The Maharajah thought it impossible. To convince himself of the truth of the assertion, he ordered the faqueer to be brought to his court, and caused him to undergo the experiment, assuring him that no precaution would be omitted to discover whether it was a deception. In consequence, the faqueer, in the presence of the court, placod himself in a complete state of *asphyxia*, having all the appearance of death.

In that state, he was wrapped in the linen on which he was sitting, theesal of Runjoot Sing was stamped thereon, and it was placed in a chest, on which the Maharajah put a strong lock. The chest was buried in a garden, outside the city, belonging to the minister, barley was sown on the ground, and the space enclosed with a wall and surrounded by sentinels. On the fortieth day, which was the time fixed for his exhumation, a great number of the authorities of the durbar, with General Ventura, and several Englishmen from the vicinity, one of them a medical man, went to the enclosure. The chest was brought up and opened, and the faqueer was found in the same position as they had left him, cold and stiff. A friend of mine told me that had I been present when they endeavoured to bring him to life, by applying warmth to the head, injecting air into his ears and mouth, and rubbing the whole of his body to promote circulation, &c., I should certainly not have had the slightest doubt of the reality of the performance. The minister, Rajah Dhyan Sing, assured me, that he himself kept this faqueer (whose name was Haridas) four months under the ground, when he was at Jummoo in the mountains. On the day of his burial, he ordered his beard to be shaved, and at his exhumation his chin was as smooth as on the day of his interment, thus furnishing a complete proof of the powers of vitality having been suspended during that period. He likewise caused himself to be interred at Jesrota, in the mountains, and at Umritsir, and also by the English in Hindostan. In the *Calcutta Medical Journal*, about 1835, there is a full description of the faqueer, and we are there informed, that he preferred having the chest, in which he was enclosed, suspended in the air, instead of its being buried beneath the earth, as he feared the possibility of his body being attacked by ants, whilst in that middle state between life and death. Having, however, refused to undergo another trial, several of the English people there doubted the truth of the story, and refused credence in so astonishing a power.* But it is quite certain that had there been any deception as regards the interment of the faqueer, rendering his experiment easy of accomplishment, those engaged or associated with him, and to whom the task of restoring the vital energies was necessarily entrusted, would, of necessity, be acquainted with the mystery, and be able, since his real decease, to emulate his example; that, however, is not the case. It appears, consequently, that the faqueer was the only one then in possession of that power; and, as a further corroboration of this view of the case, I may mention that I myself inquired in the Punjab, in the mountains and valleys of Cashmere, and in other parts of India, and made every exertion to find a person possessed of this power, in order to take him to Europe, or at least to Calcutta, but without success. Several Hindoos told me that such faqueers set no value upon money; I replied to them however, that, at all events, they fully appreciated other worldly pleasures. They did not like to hear this statement, implying that the faqueer was a *debauchee.* Several complaints had, however, been made of him, on which account Runjeet Sing intended to banish him from Lahore. He anticipated the intention, by eloping with a Katrany (woman of a Hindoo caste) to the mountains, where he died, and was burned according to the custom of the country. His elopement with this woman may serve as a proof (in contradiction to other statements) that he was neither an eunuch nor a hermaphrodite.

---

* To corroborate the above, my readers can refer to General Ventura (Paris) and also the Colonel Sir C. M. Wade (London), who were present, and assisted at the restoration of the faqueer, some accounts of whom have been published from the Colonel's statement.

Doubtless, it is a difficult task, and not within the power of every one, to acquire the skill necessary for the performance of this experiment, and those who do succeed must undergo a long and continual practice of proparatory measures. I was informed that such people have their *frænulum linguæ* cut and entirely loosened, and that they get their tongue prominent, drawing and lengthening it by means of rubbing it with butter mixed with some pellitory of Spain, in order that they may be able to lay back the tongue at the time they are about to stop respiration, so as to cover the orifice of the hinder part of the *fosses nasales*, and thus (with other means for the same purpose, which I shall mention) keep the air shut up in the body and head.* Novices, in trying the experiment, shut their eyes, and press them with their fingers, as also the cavities of the ears and nostrils, because the natural warmth of the body might cause such an expansion of the enclosed gas as otherwise to produce, by the violence of its pressure, a rupture of some of those delicate organs not yet accustomed by practice to endure it. This, I am told, is especially the case with the eyes and the tympan of the ear. For the better acquisition of this power, they are accustomed to practise the holding of the breath for a long period. They swallow a small strip of linen, in order to cleanse the stomach, and by a tube draw a quantity of water through the anus into the intestines to rinse them. This is performed while sitting in a vessel filled with water to the height of the arm-pits. It is said that the faqueer in question, a few days provious to his experiments, took some kind of purgative, and subsisted for several days on a coarse milk regimen. On the day of his

* A similar process is explained in some of the *Encyclopædias*, in the article on "Engastrimythe," or the mechanism of the ventriloquists.

burial, instead of food, he slowly swallowed, in the presence of the assembly, a rag of three fingers in breadth and thirty yards in length, and afterwards extracted it, for the purpose of removing all foreign matters from the stomach, having previously rinsed the bowels in the manner I have before mentioned. Ridiculous as this operation may appear to the reader, and as it appears, indeed, to me also, yet these artists must, of necessity, be complete masters of their body and its organism, and possess a more than ordinary power over the muscles. We are scarcely capable of swallowing a somewhat long piece of maccaroni if it is not well boiled and moistened with butter, &c., to render it palatable. It is probable, however, that they may have lost the sense of taste, and their neck-muscles may be relaxed to such a degree that the long linen strip does not meet with any resistance in the throat. These preparations being made, the faqueer stopped all the natural openings of the body with plugs of aromatic wax, placed back his tongue in the manner I have before indicated, crossed his arms over his breast, and thus suffocated himself, in the presence of a multitude of spectators. On his exhumation, one of the first operations is to draw his tongue into its natural position; after this, a warm aromatic paste, made from pulse meal, is placed on his head, and air is injected into his lungs and also through the ears, from which the plugs are withdrawn. By this operation, the pellets in the nostrils are driven out with considerable force and noise, and this is considered the first symptom of his resuscitation. Friction is then strenuously applied all over the body, and at length he begins to breathe naturally, opens his eyes, and is gradually restored to consciousness. It is related that, two hundred and fifty years ago, in the time of the Gooroo Arjun Sing, a Joghee faqueer was found in his tomb in a sitting posture, at Umritsir, and was restored to life. This faqueer is reported to have been below the ground for one hundred years; and when he revived, he related many circumstances connected with the times in which he had lived. Whether this tradition be true or false, it is impossible to say; but I am of opinion, that he, who can pass four months below the ground without becoming a prey to corruption, may also remain there for one year. Granting this, it is impossible to fix a limit to the time during which a suspension of the vital functions may continue, without injury to their subsequent power.

However paradoxical or absurd this statement may appear, and however persuaded I may be that many a reader, believing himself to be a wise man, will smile at the relation, I cannot, nevertheless, avoid confessing freely, that I do not entirely reject all the details given respecting the circumstances, for as Haller observes:—"In the interior of nature, no mortal can penetrate; happy is he who knows a small part, even of its surface." We find much credence given to such phenomena in the most ancient traditions. Who will not remember the history of Epimenides of Creta, who, after a sleep of forty years in a grotto there, is reported to have again re-entered the world from which he had so long been separated! Who will not remember also the seven holy sleepers, who, according to a Vatican manuscript, were concealed in a grotto near Ephesus, in order to escape the persecutions of the Christians, during the reign of the Emperor Decius, and who, 155 years subsequently, in the time of Theodosius II, returned to consciousness? But even rejecting these traditions, have we not also similar examples in the animal kingdom? Have not animals, especially toads, been detected in rocks, wherein, according to the calculations made, they had been enclosed for several centuries, in a state of sleep or torpor, and which animals, after having been brought into the air, have recovered their vitality; and it is not necessary to remind the naturalist of the fact, that many species of animals invariably pass the winter season in a kind of sleep, awaking in the spring with renewed and unimpaired energies. Among recent cases, which demonstrate the great endurance of human life, is the following relation:—At Vienna, some years ago, a Hungarian was, during a period of twelve months, in a comatose state, and his jaw-bones were so firmly closed that it was impossible to open his mouth; the physicians were consequently obliged to extract some of his teeth, in order to administer some remedies and broth, to preserve life; he, nevertheless, at last recovered.

In the *Philosophical Transactions* for 1705 (Nov. and Dec., Vol. XVII., p. 2177), the history of a case is related, which supports what has been previously mentioned:—"A man of about twenty-five years of age, living in the neighbourhood of Bath, fell suddenly asleep, and continued for nearly a month in that state. Two years afterwards, he was again in a similar condition: his jaw-bones closed themselves; he was unable to eat, but fell asleep, and continued to be devoid of sensation for seventeen weeks. This occurred at the time when barley was being sown, and when he again awoke it was quite ripe. In the month of August, he again fell asleep. He was bled; stimulating remedies were employed; and every means of restoration was used which the medical skill of the period could suggest, but in vain; he did not awake until the month of November." In Plott's Natural History of Oxfordshire (c. 8, sec. 11, p. 196, published in 1677), a case is alluded to, which, not being generally known, I will quote here, it being another evidence of the length of time during which a person may exist without nourishment.

"Rebekah Smith, the servant maid of one Thomas White, of Minster Lovel, being above fifty years of age, and of a robust constitution, though she seldom ate flesh (it scarcely agreeing with her), after she came from the communion on Palm-Sunday, April 16, 1671, was taken with such a dryness in her throat, that she could not swallow her spittle, nor any thing else to supply the demands of nature ; and in this state she continued, without eating or drinking, to the amazement of all, for about *ten weeks*, viz., to the 29th of June, being both St. Peter's and Witney fair day; by which time, being brought very low, her master made inquiry, and found out a person who gave him an amulet (for, it was supposed, she was bewitched) against this evil; after the application of this amulet, within two or three days (though I dare not suppose there was any connection between the medicine and the disease), she first drank a little water, then warm broths in small quantities at a time, and nothing else till Palm-Sunday again, twelve months after, when she began to eat bread and other food as she had formerly done ; and the record states that she was then about the age of sixty, and still living in the same place, ready to testify to the truth of the matter ; as were also Thomas White and his wife, who were the only other persons living in the house with her, and who would confidently assert (for they carefully observed), that they did not believe she ever took anything whatever in those *ten weeks* time, nor anything more than what is before mentioned until the expiration of the year."

The London Medical and Physical Journal, Vol. XXXV, p. 509, states that :—

" An account of the sleeping woman of Dunnibald, near Montrose, was read by the Rev. James Brewster, at the

Royal Society of Edinburgh. Her first sleeping fit lasted from the 27th to the 30th of June, 1815. Next morning she again fell into a sleep which lasted seven days, without motion, food, or evacuation. At the end of this time, by moving her hand and pointing to her mouth, it was understood she wanted food, which was given to her; but she remained in her lethargic state till the 8th of August, six weeks in all, without appearing to be awake, except on the 30th of June," &c., &c. This case is well authenticated.

And in J. N. Willan's Miscellaneous Work, published by A. Smith, M. D., p. 339, he states that he had seen many, mostly Jews and other aliens, of a dark, swarthy complexion, sometimes lie six or eight weeks in the torpid, insensible condition above described.—*Honnigberger's* "*Thirty-five years in the East*.

INTRODUCTION.

Gheraṇḍa Sanhitâ is a Tântrika work, treating of Hatha-Yoga. It consists of a dialogue between the sage Gheraṇḍa and an enquirer called Chaṇḍa Kâpâli. The book is divided into seven Lessons or Chapters and comprises, in all, some three hundred and fifty verses. It closely follows in the foot-steps of the famous treatise on Hatha-Yoga known as Hatha-Yoga Pradîpikâ. In fact, a large number of verses of Gheraṇḍa Sanhitâ correspond *verbatim* with those of the Pradîpikâ. It may, therefore, be presumed that one has borrowed from the other, or both have drawn from a common source.

The book teaches Yoga under seven heads or Sâdhanas. The first gives directions for the Purification of the Body (inside and out). The second relates to Postures, the third to Mudrâs, the fourth to Pratyâhâra, the fifth to Prâṇâyâma, the sixth to Dnyâna, and the seventh to Samâdhi. These are taught successively—a chapter being devoted to each (see Ch. I. v. 9-10-11).

The theory of Hatha-Yoga, to put it broadly, is that concentration or Samâdhi can be attained by purification of the physical body and certain physical exercises. The relation between physical shell (ghata) and mind is so complete and subtle, and their inter-action is so curious and so much enveloped in mystery, that it is not strange that Hatha-Yogis should have imagined that certain physical training will induce certain mental transformations.

Another explanation—and a later one—is that Hatha-Yoga means the Yoga or union between ha (ह) and tha (ठ) ; the ह meaning the sun ; and (ठ) the moon ; or the union of the Prâṇa and the Apâna Vâyus. This is also a physical process carried to a higher plane.

The first question, which an unprejudiced enquirer will naturally put, after perusing this book, will be, are all these things possible? and do these practices produce the result attributed to them ?

As to the possibility of these practices, there can be no doubt. They do not violate any anatomical or physiological facts. The practices, some of them at least, may appear revolting and disgusting, but they are not *per se* impossible. Moreover, many of my readers may have come across persons who can practically illustrate these. Such persons are by no means rare in India. Every place of pilgrimage, such as Benares and Allahabad, contains several of them, in various stages of progress. My own Guru showed me and all his visitors at Allahabad and Meerut several of these processes, and taught some people how to do them themselves. The difficult processes, such as Vâri-Sâra (Ch. I. 17), Agni-Sâra (I. 20), Danda-Dhauti (I. 37), Vâsa Dhauti (I. 40), &c., were all shown by him ; so also the various Vastis, Neti-Âsanas, &c. Many of these may be classified as gymnastic exercises ; their performers need not always be holy or saint-like personages. Several jugglers have been known to perform various Âsanas, and Mudrâs, and earn their livelihood by showing them to the public. For persons whose muscles have become stiffened and the bones hardened by age, the acquirement of several of these postures, &c., is next to impossible ; and it is better that they should not court failure or disappointment by attempting these at an advanced age. But Prâṇâyâma (regulation of breath) Dhâraṇâ and Dhyâna are possible for all.

As to the utility of these processes, genuine doubts may be entertained. Many of them may appear puerile, and, if not positively injurious, at least, useless. Although it is not possible within the short space at my command, to give the rationale of *all* these practices, and to justify them to a doubting public, I shall briefly illustrate the advantages of some of them. Thus, to begin with वातसार (I. 15). It is the process of filling the stomach with air, and expelling the wind through the posterior passage. The greatest duct or canal in the human body is the alimentary canal beginning with the œsophagus (throat) and ending with the rectum. It is some twenty-six feet in length. This great drain contains all the rubbish of the body. Nature periodically cleanses it. Yoga practice makes that cleansing thorough and voluntary. If the cleansing is incomplete, then the fœtid matters putrify in the stomach and intestines, and generate noxious and deleterious gases which cause diseases. Now वातसार, by passing a current of air through the canal, causes the oxidation of the fœtid products of the body ; and thus conduces to health, and increases digestion. In fact, it gives a tone to the whole system. Similarly, वारिसार is flushing the canal with water, instead of air. It thoroughly purges the whole canal; and does the same work as an aperient or a purgative, but with ten times more efficacy and without the injurious effects of these drugs. A person, knowing Vâtasâra and Vârisâra, stands in no need of purgatives: the same may be said of Bahiskrita Dhauti (I. 22). By Agnisâra (I. 20), the nerves and muscles of the stomach are brought under the control of volition; and by the gentle shaking of the stomach and the intestines, these organs lose their lethargy, and act with greater vigour. The washing taught in I. 23, 24, is a little dangerous, and may lead to prolapsus, and, a person who can do वारिसार need not do this. The advantages of cleaning the teeth and the tongue are obvious, and need not be dilated upon. The lengthening of the tongue (I. 32) is necessary for performing hybernation. In doing this, man but imitates the lower creation like frogs, &c., who in hybernating turn their tongues upward, closing the respiratory passage. Perhaps, the most interesting of all Dhautis is the Vâsa-Dhauti (I. 41), which has led unobservant persons to the belief that the Yogîs can bring out the intestines by the mouth, wash them, and then swallowing them again place them in their proper position. This Dhauti is, however, a very simple process, and by so doing the mucus, phlegm, &c., adhering to the sides of the alimentary canal are removed. Water and air could not remove these viscid substances that stick to the sides of the canal.

The Neti, an easy process, clears the nostrils;

and cures the tendency or predisposition to cold and catarrh. The Kapâlabhâti (1.55) is a means of cleansing the frontal sinus, said to be the seat of Intelligence. This hollow cannot be directly reached from the outside, but by this process of Kâpalbhâti, the nerves surrounding it and spreading over the fore-head are brought into play and invigorated.

The various Âsanas taught in Chapter II. are gymnastic exercises, good for general health, and peace of mind and calming of passions. The thirty-two Âsanas taught in this book are not all of equal efficacy or importance. Padmâsana is generally approved by all. The others may be practised occasionally for variation and recreation. Some of these postures help in checking animal passions by causing atrophy of the nerves of particular places. Others by straining and stretching of certain muscules create a pleasant sensation of strength and refreshment. The Âsanas are antidotes to the sedentary contemplation of Yoga—a habit which may otherwise lead to mental hallucinations and nervous disorders.

The Mudrâs are similar to Âsanas in their action and efficacy. The gazing taught in some of these induces hypnotic sleep ; and the Bandhas by closing all the exits for air, produce a tension within the system, generating thereby a sort of electric current or force called Kuṇḍalinî S'akti. It is this S'akti which is the help-mate of the Yogîs in performing their wonders. The Khecharî Mudrâ (III. 25-27) causes levitation of the body. That levitation is possible has now been established beyond doubt. What the particular conditions are, under which this takes place, has not yet been fully investigated by Western Science: but that the restraining of breath is one of these conditions may be said to be an undoubted truth. The S'akti-châlana is a mysterious process, and until a person practically realises it, he can hardly believe it. The Mudrâs are mixed physical and mental processes, a bridge between Âsanas and Pratyâhâra.

The subject of Pratyâhâra is treated in Chapter IV in five ślokas. It is the process of restraining the mind from wandering, and restricting it to a fixed idea. All the five senses must be controlled, and they should not be allowed to divert the attention.

Prâṇâyâma is the Hatha-Yoga *par excellence.* It is as dangerous when practised without the supervision of a competent teacher, as it is useful when practised under his supervision. To quote the words of a great authority on this subject: "By practising it according to rule, all diseases are destroyed; but by doing so irregularly, all diseases are generated such as hiccough, asthma, cough, head-ache, ear-ache, diseases of the eye &c." A practical Guru is absolutely necessary to teach Prâṇâyâma, the directions given in this book are useful as subsidiary rules. Many mistakes and dangers will, however, be warded off by a strict adherence to these rules. The place—a small and solitary cell; the time—spring and autumn; the food—light and sâtwika: these are some of the important preliminaries. Over-exertion, fasting, &c., should be avoided (V. 30.) This shows clearly that Hatha-Yoga is not to be confounded with asceticism. It is far from that. As the training of an athlete is not asceticism; so that of a Hatha-Yogî is far from being so. True, celibacy is a necessary condition for both, but then that alone does not constitute asceticism. The directions regarding food are peculiar for the people of Bengal, the author of this treatise being apparently a Vaishṇava of Bengal. For other countries and persons, these directions may not be applicable in their entirety. But animal food, intoxicating liquors, tobacco, and drugs are strictly prohibited for all climes.

There are three parts of Prâṇâyâma:—Pûraka or drawing in of the breath; Kumbhaka or retaining the breath; and Rechaka or expelling the breath. The proportion of these should be 1: 4: 2, *i.e.*, if Pûraka takes 12 seconds, Kumbhaka should be 48 seconds, and Rechaka 24 seconds. The ratio being kept the same, the period of retention, &c., may be increased *ad infinitum.* The beginner should proceed cautiously, and should not increase the periods of 16: 64: 32 seconds. He should carefully note the various mental and physical changes going on in his system while practising it. Perspiration should be wiped off with a dry towel: nor should he be afraid when he begins to feel a sort of quiver all over the body. Sometimes he may be jerked off his seat, sometimes he may involuntarily jump about the room like a frog. These should not frighten him. Sometimes there may be no physical manifestations, but mental reactions. He may hear noises, see visions, smell strange odours, or taste delightful delicacies. These are for the most part hallucinations, indicating an excited state of the nervous system. These will soon go off of themselves when not attended to. But flashes of truth will also illumine his heart now and then. Sometimes in the Chidâkâśa, he may see reflected distant scenes and events, thoughts of persons will become visible to him ; and he himself may leave his body and be carried in space with incalculable velocity. All these symptoms accompany Prâṇâyâma. The Guru must always be near at hand to help and control; for otherwise insanity and not clairvoyance may be the outcome of all this. These are the results of higher stages of Prâṇâyâma. But every person may practise this for two or three minutes, and experience its beneficial results on his own body. Petty disorders like head-ache, stomach-ache, chill before fever, weariness of body and mind will vanish instantaneously by performing two or three Kumbhakas. Some persons are born with the faculty of performing Prâṇâyâma—Swedenbourg was a living example of this in the West. All persons unconciously perform Prâṇâyâma when absorbed in deep thinking.

The ten Vâyus (V. 60) are the various nervous forces or currents of the human body. Five of them Prâṇa, &c., belong (according to some) not to the physical body, but to the subtle or S'ukshma S'arîra. The six lotuses or Chakras do not belong to the physical body, but are centres of force in the Sûkshma S'arîra. The Sûkshma S'arîra being an exact duplicate of the physical body, but being ethereal is hardly a subject of physical demonstration. The five Vâyus, Nâga, &c. (V. 62), however, belong to the physical body and regulate the physiological functions of the material system.

The various sorts of Kumbhakas taught in Chapter V. do not require much elucidation. The Bhrâmarî Kumbhaka (V. 77), however, is a little peculiar. It leads one to hear the various sounds called Anâhata. These sounds are said to be caused within the body by the rushing of the blood through the arteries and veins. The fixing of mind on these sounds soon produces trance.

Dhyâna and Samâdhi are purely mental processes. Fixity and one-pointedness of attention produce trance. The experiments of hypnotism prove this. To fix the mind on one idea produces exaltation of mental faculties.

GHAZIPUR,
7th September 1893. } S. C. V.

THE YOGA SAMHITA.

A TREATISE ON HATHA YOGA

BY

GHERANDA MUNI.

1. Once Chanda Kapâli went to the hermitage of Gheranda Muni, and, having saluted him with meekness and devotion,

CHANDA KAPALI SAID :—

2. O Yogeswar ! O Yogesh ! O Lord ! I wish now to hear Ghatasthayoga (Physiological yoga) which is the cause of Tatwadnyâna (knowledge of truth).

GHERANDA REPLIED :—

3. Well asked, indeed, O brave one : I shall tell thee what thou hast asked me. O son ! preserve it with deligence.

4. There is no bond like that of Mâyâ (delusion), there is no force stronger than Yoga, there is no friend truer than Knowledge, and there is no enemy worse than Pride.

5. As by practice and knowledge of the alphabets, all sciences can be learned, so by first practising Yoga one attains by degrees the knowledge of the truth (Tatwadnyâna).

6. From good and bad works the Ghatas (or bodies) of men are produced, and the body gives

birth to Karma (or works) and thus the circle is continued like a rotating mill.

7. As the Ghati-yantra (a rotating mill) revolves up and down, moved by bullocks, so the Jiva (human soul) passes through life and death moved by Karma.

8. As an unbaked earthen pot is soon dissolved when placed in water, so the body; it must be strengthened and purified by the fire of Yoga in order to harden it.

THE SEVEN SÂDHANAS OR PRACTICES.

9. The seven practices or Sâdhanas which appertain to Yoga are the following :—Purification, strengthening, steadiness, calmness, lightness, perception, and isolation.

10—12. 1st—S'odhan or purification is done by the six Karmas (to be mentioned shortly); 2nd—Âsana or posture gives Driddhatâ or strength ; 3rd—Mudrâ gives Sthiratâ or steadiness ; 4th—Pratyâhâr gives Dhairyatâ or courage or calmness ; 5th—Prânâyâma gives lightness or Laghimâ ; 6th—Dhyâna gives perception (Pratyakshatwa) of self ; and 7th—Samâdhi gives isolation (Nirliptatâ), which is verily emancipation.

THE S'ODHANAS OR PURIFICATION.

13. (1) Dhouti ; (2) Basti ; (3) Neti ; (4) Lonkiki, (5) Trâtaka, (6) Kapâlabhâti are the Shatkarmas or six practices known as S'odhana.

1.—DHOUTI.

14. Dhouti is of four kinds, and they clear away the impurities of the body. They are:—(*a*) Antar-

dhouti (internal washing); (*b*) Dantdhouti (cleaing the teeth); (*c*) Hriddhouti (cleaning the heart); (*d*) Mulashodhana (cleaning the Anus).

ANTAR-DHOUTI.

15. Antardhouti is again sub-divided into four parts :—Vâtâsar (wind purification), Vârisar (water purification), Vahnisar (fire purification), and Bahiskrita.

VÂTÂSARA-DHOUTI.

16. Contract the mouth like the beak of a crow and drink air slowly, and fill the stomach slowly with it, and move it therein, and then slowly force it out through the lower passage.

17. The Vatasar is a very secret process, it causes the purification of the body, it destroys all diseases and increases the gastric-fire.

VÂRISARA-DHOUTI.

18. Fill the mouth with water down to the throat, and then drink it slowly ; and then move it through the stomach forcing it downwards expelling it through the rectum.

19. This process should be kept very secret. It purifies the body. And by practising it with care one gets a luminous or shining body.

20. The Vârisara is the highest Dhouti. He who practises it with ease purifies his filthy body and turns it into a shining one.

AGNISARA OR FIRE PURIFICATION.

21. Press in the navel knot or intestines towards the spine for one hundred times. This is

Agnisâr or fire process. This gives success in the practice of Yoga, it cures all the diseases of and increases the fire of the stomach (gastric juice.)

22. This form of Dhouti should be kept very secret, and it is hardly to be attained even by the gods. By this Dhauti alone one certainly gets a luminous body.

Bahiskrita-Dhouti.

23. By Kâkachancha or crow-bill Mudrâ fill the stomach with air, hold it there for one hour and a half, and then force it down towards the intestines. This Dhouti must be kept a great secret, and must not be revealed to any body.

24. Then standing in navel-deep water, draw out the Saktinadi (long intestines), wash the Nadi with hand, and so long as its filth is not all washed away, wash it with care, and then draw it in again into the abdomen.

25. This process should be kept secret. It is not easily to be attained even by the gods, simply by this Dhouti one gets Deva-deha (Godlike body.)

26. As long as a person has not the power of retaining the breath for an hour and a half (or retaining wind in the stomach for that period) so long he cannot achieve this grand Dhouti or purification known as Bahiskritadhauti.

2.—Danta-Dhouti or Teeth Purification.

27. Danta-Dhouti is of five kinds: purification of the teeth, of the root of the tongue, of the two holes of the ear, and of the frontal-senews.

Danta-Mula-Dhouti.

28. Rub the teeth with catechu-powder or with pure earth so long as dental impurities are not removed.

29. This teeth-washing is a great Dhouti and an important process in the practice of Yoga for the Yogis. It should be done daily in the morning by the Yogis, in order to preserve the teeth. In purification this is approved of by the Yogis.

Jivhâ S'odhana or Tongue-Dhouti.

30. I shall now tell you the method of cleansing the tongue. The elongation of the tongue destroys old age, death and disease.

31. Join together the three fingers known as the index, the middle and the ring finger, put them into the throat, and rub well and clean the root of the tongue and by washing it again, throw out the phlegm.

32. Having thus washed it, rub it with butter, and milk it again and again; then by holding the tip of the tongue with an iron instrument pull it out slowly and slowly.

33. Do this daily with deligence before the rising and setting sun. By so doing the tongue becomes elongated.

Karna-Dhouti or Ear-cleaning.

34. Clean the two holes of the ears by the index and the ring fingures. By practising it daily the mystical sounds are heard.

KAPÂLA-RANDHRA-DHOUTI.

35. Rub with the thumb of the right hand the depression in the forehead near the bridge of the nose. By the practice of this Yoga, diseases arising from derangements of phlegmatic humours are cured.

36. The vessels become purified and clairvoyance is induced. This should be practised daily after awakening from sleep, after meals, and in the evening.

HRID-DHOUTI.

37. Hrid-Dhauti or purification of heart is of three kinds, *viz.*, by Danda (a stick), Vamana (vomiting), and by Vastra (cloth).

DANDA-DHOUTI.

38. Take either a plantain stalk or a stalk of (Haridra) turmeric, or a stalk of cane, and thrust it slowly into the æsophagus and then draw it out slowly.

39. By this process all the phlegm, bile and other impurities are expelled out of the mouth. By this Danda-Dhouti every kind of heart-disease is surely cured.

VAMANA-DHOUTI.

40. After meal let the wise practitioner drink water full up to the throat, then looking for a short while upwards, let him vomit it out again. By daily practising this Yoga, disorders of phlegm and bile are cured.

VASTRA-DHOUTI.

41. Let him swallow slowly a thin cloth, four

fingers wide, then let him draw it out again. This is called Vastra-Dhouti.

42. This cures Gulma or abdominal diseases, fever, enlarged spleen, leprosy, and other skin diseases and disorders of phlegm and bile, and day by day the practitioner gets health, strength, and cheerfulness.

Mula S'odhana or Purification of Anus.

43. The Apânavâyu does not flow freely so long as the anus is not purified. Therefore with the greatest care let him practise this purification of the anus.

44. By the stalk of the root of Haridra (turmeric) or the middle finger, the anus should be carefully cleansed with water over and over again.

45. This destroys constipation, indigestion, and dyspepsia, and increases the beauty and vigour of the body and enkindles the sphere of the fire (*i. e.* the gastric juice).

End of Dhoutis.

PARTS II.

BASTIS.

46. The Bastis are described of two kinds, *viz*: Jala Basti (or water Basti) and Sukshma Basti (or dry Basti). Water Basti is done in water and dry Basti always on land.

Jala-Basti.

47. Entering water up to the navel and assuming the posture called Utkatâsana, let him contract

and dilate the sphincter-muscle of the anus. This is called Jala-Basti.

48. This cures Prameha (urinary disorders), Gudâvarta (disorders of wind) and Krurvâyu (disorders of the wind). His body becomes free from all diseases and becomes as beautiful as that of the god Cupid.

STHALA-BASTI.

49. Assuming the posture called Paschimtâna let him move the intestines slowly downwards, then contract and dilate the sphincter-muscle of the anus with Aswini-Mudra.

50. By this practice of Yoga constipation never occurs and it increases gastric fire and cures flatulence.

End of Basti-Karma.

PART III.

NETI.

51. Take a thin thread measuring half a cubit and insert it into the nostrils, and passing it through, pull it out by the mouth. This is called Neti-Kriya.

52. By practising the Neti-Kriya, one obtains Khechari Siddhi. It destroys the disorders of phlegm and produces clairvoyance or clear sight.

PART IV.

LOUKIKI-YOGA.

53. With great force move the stomach and intestines from one side to the other. This is called Loukiki-Yoga. This destroys all diseases and increases the bodily fire.

PART V.

TRÂTAKA OR GAZING.

54. Gaze (look) steadily without wincking at any small object until tears begin to flow. This is called Trâtaka by the wise.

55. By practising this Yoga, S'ambhavi Siddhis are obtained; and certainly all diseases of the eye are destroyed and clairvoyance is induced.

PART VI.

KAPÂLABHÂTI.

56. Kapâlabhâti is of three kinds: Vyût-krama Vâma-krama, and S'it-krama. They destroy disorders of phlegm.

VÂMA-KRAMA.

57. Draw the wind through the left nostril and expel it through the right, and draw it again through the right and expel it through the left.

58. This inspiration and expiration must be done without any force. This practice destroys disorders of phlegm.

VYÛT-KRAMA.

59. Draw the water through the two nostrils and expel it through the mouth slowly and slowly. This is called Vyût-krama which destroys disorders of phlegm.

S'IT-KRAMA.

60. Suck water through the mouth and expel it through the nostrils. By this practice of Yoga one becomes like the god Cupid.

61. Old age never comes to him and decrepitude never disfigures him. The body becomes healthy, elastic, and disorders of phlegm are destroyed.

End of the first lesson.

SECOND LESSON.

THE ASANAS OR POSTURES.

Gheranda said :—There are eighty-four Lakhs of Âsanâs described by Shiva. These postures being as many in number as there are numbers of species of living creatures in this universe.

2. Among them eighty-four are the best; and among these eighty-four, thirty-two have been found useful for mankind in this world.

Different kinds of Postures.

3—6. The thirty-two Âsanas that give perfection in this mortal world are the following :—

1. Siddham (*perfect posture*).
2. Padmam (*Lotus posture*).
3. Bhadram (*Gentle posture*).
4. Muktam (*Free posture*).
5. Vajram (*Adamant posture*).
6. Swastika (*Prosperous posture*).
7. Sivham (*Lion posture*).
8. Gomukha (*Cow-mouth posture*).
9. Vira (*Heroic posture*).
10. Dhanur (*Bow posture*).
11. Mritam (*Corpse posture*).
12. Guptam (*Hidden posture*).
13. Matsyam (*Fish posture*).

14. Matsendra.
15. Goraksha.
16. Paschimtàna.
17. Utkatam.
18. S'akatam (*Dangerous posture*).
19. Mayuram (*Peacock posture*).
20. Kukkutam (*Cock posture*).
21. Kurma (*Tortoise posture*).
22. Uttan Manduka.
23. Utten Kurmakam.
24. Vriksha (*Free posture*).
25. Manduka (*Frog posture*).
26. Garuda.
27. Vrisham (*Bull posture.*)
28. Salabha.
29. Makara.
30. Ushtram (*Camel posture*).
31. Bhujangam (*Snake posture*).
32. Yoga.

1.—Siddhâsana.

7—8. The practitioner who has subdued his passions, having placed one hill at the anal aperture should keep the other heel on the root of the generative organ; afterwards should affix his chin upon the chest, and being quiet and straight, gaze at the spot between the two eye-brows. This is called Siddh-âsana and leads to emancipation.

2.—Padmâsana.

9. Place the right foot on the left thigh and similarly the left one on the right thigh, also cross the hands behind the back and firmly catch hold of the great toes of feet so crossed. Place the

chin on the chest and fix the gaze on the tip of the nose. This posture is called Padmâsana (or Lotus posture). This posture destroys all diseases.

3.—Bhadrâsana.

10—11. Place the heels crosswise under the testes attentively ; cross the hands behind the back and take hold of the toes of the feet. Fix the gaze on the tip of the nose, having previously adopted the Mudra called Jalandhara. This is Bhadrâsana (or happy posture) which destroys all sorts of diseases.

4.—Muktâsana.

12. Place the left heel at the root of the organ of generation and the right heel above that, place the head and the neck straight with the body. This posture is called Muktâsana. It gives Siddhi (perfection).

5.—Vajrâsana or Adamant posture.

13. Make the thighs tight like adamant and place the legs by the two sides of the anus. This is called Vajrâsana. It gives psychic powers to the Yogi.

6.—Swastikâsana.

14. Drawing the legs and thighs together and placing the feet underneath them, keeping the body in its easy condition and sitting straight, constitute the posture called Swastikâsana.

7.—Simhâsana.

15—16. The two heels to be placed under the scrotum contrariwise (*i. e.*, left heel on the right side and the right heel on the left side of it) and turned upwards, the knees to be placed on the ground, (and the hands placed on the knees), mouth to be kept open ; practising the Jâlandhara mudrâ one should fix his gaze on the tip of the nose. This is Simhâsana (Lion-posture), the destroyer of all diseases.

8.—GOMUKHÂSANA.

17. The two feet to be placed on the ground, and the heels to be placed contrariwise under the buttocks ; the body to be kept steady and the mouth raised, and sitting equably; this is called Gomukhâsana : resembling the mouth of a cow.

9.—VÎRÂSANA.

18. One leg (the right foot) to be placed on the other (left) thigh, and the other foot to be turned backwards : This is called Vîrâsana (hero-posture).

10.—DHANURÂSANA.

19. Spreading the legs on the ground, straight like a stick, and catching hold of (the toes of) the feet with the hands, and making the body bent like a bow is called by the Yogîs Dhanurâsana or Bow-posture.

11.—MRITÂSANA.

20. Lying flat on the ground like a corpse is called Mritâsana (the Corpse-posture). This posture destroys fatigue, and quiets the agitation of the mind.

12.—GUPTÂSANA.

21. Hide the two feet under the two knees, and place the anus on the feet. This is known as Guptâsana (Hidden-posture).

13.—Matsyâsana.

22. Make the Padmâsana-posture (as stated in verse 9) without the crossing of the arms; lie on the back, holding the head by the two elbows. This is Matsyâsana (Fish-posture), destroyer of diseases.

14.—Paschimatâna-Âsana.

23. Spread the two legs on the ground stiff like a stick (the heels not touching), and place the fore-head on the two knees, and catch with the hands the toes. This is called Paschimatâna-Âsana.

15.—Matsyendrâsana.

24—25. Keeping the abdominal region at ease like the back, bending the left leg, place it on the right thigh; then place on this the elbow of the right hand, and place the face on the palm of the right hand, and fix the gaze between the eye-brows. This is called Matsyendra posture.

16.—Gorakshâsana.

26—27. Between the knees and the thighs, the two feet turned upward and placed in a hidden way, the heels being carefully covered by the two hands out-stretched; the throat being contracted, let one fix the gaze on the tip of the nose. This is called Gorakshâsana. It gives success to the Yogîs.

17.—Utkatâsana.

28. Let the toes touch the ground, and the heels be raised in the air, place the anus on the heels: this is known as *Utkatâsana*.

18.—S'akatâsana.

29. Placing the left foot and the leg on the

ground, surround the left foot by the right leg; and place the two hands on the two knees. This is S'akatâsana.

19.—Mayûrâsana.

30—31. Place the palms of the two hands on the ground, place the umbilical region on the two elbows, stand upon the hands, the legs being raised in the air, and crossed like Padmâsana. This is called Mayûrâsana (Peacock Posture). The Peacock-posture destroys the effects of unwholesome food; it produces heat in the stomach; it destroys the effects of deadly poisons; it easily cures diseases like Gulma and fever; such is this useful Posture.

20.—Kukkutâsana.

32. Sitting on the ground, cross the legs in Padmâsana posture, thrust down the hands between the thighs and the knees, stand on the hands, supporting the body on the elbows. This is called Cock-posture.

21.—Kûrmâsana.

33. Place the heels contrariwise under the scrotum, stiffen (or keep at ease) the head, neck and body. This is called Tortoise posture.

22.—Uttâna Kûrmâsana.

34. Assume the cock-posture (as stated in verse 32), catch hold of the neck with the hands, and stand stretched like a tortoise. This is Uttâna Kûrmâsana.

23.—Mandukâsana.

35. Carry the feet towards the back, the toes touching each other, and place the knees forwards. This is called the Frog-posture.

24.—Uttâna Mandukâsana.

36. Assume the Frog-posture (as in verse 35), hold the head by the elbows, and stand up like a frog. This is called Uttâna Mandukâsana.

25.—Vrikshâsana.

37. Stand straight on one leg (the left), bending the right leg, and placing the right foot on the root of the left thigh ; standing thus like a tree on the ground is called the Tree-posture.

26.—Garudâsana.

38. Place the legs and the thigh on the ground pressing it, steady the body with the two knees, place the two hands on the knees ; this is called Garuda-posture.

27.—Vrishâsana.

39. Place the anus on the right heel, on the left of it place the left leg crossing it opposite way, and touch the ground. This is called Bull-posture.

28.—S'alabhâsana.

40. Lie on the ground face dwnwards, the two hands being placed on the chest, touching the ground with the palms, raise the legs in the air one cubit high. This is called Locust-posture.

29.—Makarâsana.

41. Lie on the ground face downwards, the chest touching the earth, the two legs being stretched : catch the head with the two arms. This is Makarâsana, increaser of the bodily heat.

30.—Ushtrâsana.

42. Lie on the ground face downwards, turn up the legs and place them towards the back, catch the legs with the hands, contract forcibly the mouth and the abdomen. This is called the camel-posture.

31.—Bhujangâsana.

43—44. Let the body, from the navel downwards to the toes, touch the ground, place the palms on the ground, raise the head (the upper portion of the body) like a serpent. This is called Serpent-posture. This always increases the bodily heat, destroys all diseases, and by the practice of this posture the serpent-Goddess (the kuṇḍaliṇi force) awakes.

32.—Yogâsana.

45—46. Turn the feet upwards, place them on the knees; then place the hands on the ground with the palms turned upwards; inspire and fix the gaze on the tip of the nose. This is called Yoga-posture, assumed by the Yogîs when practising Yoga.

THIRD LESSON.

ON MUDRÂS.

Gheranda said :—1—3. There are twenty-five mudrâs, the practice of which gives success to the Yogîs. They are :—

(1) Mahâ-mudrâ, (2) Nabho-mudrâ, (3) Uddîyâna (4) Jâlandhara (5) Mûlabandha (6) Mahâbandha (7) Mahâvedha (8) Khecharî, (9) Viparîtakarî, (10)

Yoni, (11) Vajroṇî, (12) Sáktichâlanî, (13) Tadâgî, (14) Mândavî, (15) S'âmbhavî, (16) Pancha-dhâraṇâ (five dhâraṇâs), (21) Aśvinî, (22) Pâśinî (23) Kâkî, (24) Mâtangî and (25) Bhujanginî.

The Advantages of Practising Mudrâs.

4—5. Maheśwara when addressing his consort, has recited the advantages of Mudrâs in these words : "O Devi ! I have told you all the Mudrâs ; their knowledge leads to adeptship. It should be kept secret with great care, and should not be taught indiscriminately to every one. This gives happiness to the Yogîs, and is not to be easily attained by the maruts (gods of air) even."

1.—Mahâmudrâ.

6—7. Pressing carefully the anus by the left heel, stretch the right leg, and take hold of the toe by the hand ; contract the throat (not expelling the breath) and fix the gaze between the eye-brows. This is called Mahâ-mudrâ by the wise.

Its benefits.

8. The practice of Mahâ-mudrâ cures consumption, obstruction of the bowels, the enlargement of spleen, the indigestion and fever—in fact it cures all diseases.

2.—Nabho-Mudrâ.

9. In whatever business a Yogî may be engaged, wherever he may be, let him always keep his tongue turned upwards (towards the soft palate), and restrain the breath. This is called Nabho-Mudrâ ; it destroys all the diseases of the Yogi.

3.—Uddîyâna-Bandha.

10. Contract the bowels equably above and below the navel towards the back, so that the abdominal viscera may touch the back. He who practises this Uddîyâna (Flying up), without ceasing, conquers death. The Great Bird (Breath), by this process, is instantly forced up into the Sushumṇá, and flies (moves) constantly therein only.

Its benefits.

11. Of all Bandhanas, this is the best. Complete practice of this makes emancipation easy.

4.—Jâlandhara.

12. Contracing the throat, place the chin on the chest. This is called Jâlandhara. By this Bandha the sixteen Âdhâras are closed. This and the Mahâ-mudrâ destroy death.

Its benefits.

13. The Jâlandhara is a success-giving and well-tried Bandha; he who practises it for six months becomes an adept without doubt.

5.—Mûlabandha.

14—15. Press with the heel of the left foot the region between the anus and the scrotum, and contract the rectum; carefully press the intestines near the navel on the spine; and put the right heel on the organ of generation or pubes. This is called Mûlabandha, destroyer of decay.

Its benefits.

16—17. The person who desires to cross the

ocean of Existence, let him go to a retired place, and practise in secresy this Mudrâ. By the practice of it, the Vâyu (Prâṇa) is controlled undoubtedly; let one silently practise this, without laziness, and with care.

6.—Mahâbandha.

18—19. Close the anal orifice by the heel of the left foot, press that heel with the right foot carefully, move slowly and slowly the muscles of the rectum, and slowly contract the muscles of the yoni or perineum (space between anus and organ): restrain the breath by Jâlandhara. This is called Mahâbandha.

Its benefits.

20. The Mahâbandha is the Greatest Bandha, it destroys decay and death: by virtue of this Bandha a man accomplishes all his desires.

7.—Mahâvedha.

21—22. As the beauty, youth and charms of women are in vain without men; so are Mûlabandha, and Mahâbandha without Mahâvedha. Sit first in Mahâbandha posture, then restrain breath by Uddâna Kumbhaka. This is called Mahâvedha—the giver of success to the Yogîs.

Its benefits.

23—24. The Yogî who daily practises Mahâbandha, and Mûlabandha accompanied with Mahâvedha, is the best of the Yogîs. For him there is no fear of death, and decay does not approach him: this Vedha should be kept carefully secret by the Yogîs.

8.—Khecharî Mudrâ.

25. Cut down the lower tendon of the tongue, and move the tongue constantly : rub it with fresh butter, and draw it out (to lengthen it) with an iron instrument.

N.B.—This is the preliminary to Khecharî Mudrâ. Its object is so to lengthen the tongue, that when drawn out it may touch with its tip the space between the eye-brows. This can be done by cutting away the lower tendon. It takes about three years to cut away the whole tendon. I saw my Guru doing it in this wise. On every Monday he used to cut the tendon one-twelfth of an inch deep and sprinkle salt over it so that the cut portions may not join together. Then rubbing the tongue with butter he used to pull it out. Peculiar iron instruments are employed for this purpose; the painful process is repeated every week till the tongue can be stretched out to the requisite length.

26. By practising this always, the tongue becomes long, and when it reaches the space between the two eyebrows, then the Khecharî is accomplished.

27. Then (the tongue being lengthened) practise turning it upwards and backwards so as to touch the palate, till at length it reaches the holes of the nostrils opening into the mouth. Close those holes with the tongue (thus stopping inspiration), and fix the gaze on the space between the two eyebrows. This is called Khecharî.

Its benefits.

28. By this practice there is neither fainting, nor hunger, nor thirst, nor laziness. There comes neither disease nor decay nor death. The body becomes divine.

29. The body cannot be burned by fire, nor dried up by the air, nor wetted by water, nor bitten by snakes.

30. The body becomes beautiful; Samâdhi is verily attained, and the tongue touching the holes obtains various juices (it drinks nectar).

31—32. Various juices being produced, day by day the man experiences new sensations; first, he experiences a saltish taste, then alkaline, then bitter, then astringent, then he feels the taste of butter, then of ghee, then of milk, then of curd, then of whey, then of honey, then of palm juice, and lastly arises the taste of nectar.

9.—Viparîtakaraṇî.

33—35. The sun (the solar Nâdî) dwells at the root of the navel, and the moon at the root of the palate; the process by which the sun is brought upward and the moon carried downward is called Viparîtakaraṇî. It is a secret Mudrâ in all the Tantras. Place the head on the ground, with hands spread, raise the legs up, and thus remain steady. This is called Viparîta-karaṇî.

Its benefits.

36. By the constant practice of this Mudrâ, decay and death are destroyed. He becomes an adept, and does not perish even at Pralaya.

10.—Yonimudrâ.

37—42. Sitting in Siddhâsana, close the two ears with the two thumbs, the eyes with the index fingers, the nostrils with the middle fingers, the upper lip with the fore fingers, and the lower lip with the little fingers. Draw in the Prâṇa-Vâyu by Kâkî mudrâ, (as in verse 86) and join it with the Apâna-vâyu; contemplating the six chakras in their order, let the wise one awaken the sleeping serpent-Goddess Kundalini, by repeating the mantra Huṇ (हुं), and Haṇsa (हंस:), and raising the S'akti (Force-kuṇdali) with the jîva, place them at the thousand-petalled lotus. Being himself full of S'akti, being joined with the great S'iva, let him think of the various pleasures and enjoyments. Let him contemplate on the union of S'iva (spirit) and S'akti (Force or energy) in this world. Being himself all bliss, let him realise that he is the Brahma. This Yoni-mudrâ is a great secret, difficult to be obtained even by the Devas. By once obtaining perfection in its practice, one enters verily into Samâdhi.

Its benefits.

43—44. By the practice of this Mudrâ, one is never polluted by the sins of killing a Brâhmaṇa, killing a fœtus, drinking liquour, or polluting the bed of the Preceptor. All the mortal sins and the venal sins are completely destroyed by the practice of this Mudrâ. Let him therefore practise it, if he wishes for emancipation.

11.—Vajroṇî Mudrâ.

45. Place the two palms on the ground, raise the legs in the air upward, the head not touching the earth. This awakens the S'akti, causes long life, and is called Vajroṇî by the sages.

Its benefits.

46—48. This practice is the highest of Yogas; it causes emancipation, and this beneficial Yoga gives perfection to the Yogîs. By virtue of this Yoga, the Bindu-Siddhi (retention of seed) is obtained, and when that Siddhi is obtained what else can he not attain in this world. Though immersed in manifold pleasures, if he practises this Mudrâ, he attains verily all perfections.

12.—S'AKTI CHÂLANÎ.

49. The great goddess Kundalinî, the energy of of Self, âtma-śakti (spiritual force), sleeps in the Mûlâdhâra (rectum); she has the form of a serpent having three coils and a half.

50. So long as she is asleep in the body, the Jîva is like a brute, and true knowledge does not arise though he may practise ten millions of Yoga.

51. As by a key, a door is opened, so by awakening the Kundalinî by Hatha Yoga, the door of Brahmâ is unclocked.

52. Encircling the loins with a piece of cloth, seated in a secret room, not naked in an outer room, let him practise the S'akti-châlana.

53. One cubit long, and four fingers (3 inches) wide, should be the encircling cloth, soft, white and of fine texture. Join this cloth with the Kati-Sûtra (a string worn round the loin).

54—55. Rub the body with ashes, sit in Siddhâsana-posture, drawing the Prâṇa-Vâyu with the nostrils, forcibly join it with the Apâna. Contract the rectum slowly by the Aśvinî Mudrâ, so long as the Vâyu does not enter the Sushumṇâ, and manifest its presence.

56. By restraining the breath by Kumbhaka in this way, the Serpent Kundalinî, feeling suffocated awakes and rises upwards to the Brahmarandhra.

57. Without the Sáktichâlana, the Yoni-Mûdrâ is not complete or perfected; first the Châlana should be practised and then the Yoni-Mudrâ should be learnt.

58. O Chaṇda-kâpâli! thus have I taught thee the S'aktichâlana. Preserve it with care: and practise it daily.

Its benefits.

59. This mudrâ should be kept carefully concealed. It destroys decay and death. Therefore the Yogî, desirous of perfection, should practise it.

60. The Yogî who practises this daily, acquires adeptship, attains Vigraha-siddhi and all his diseases are cured.

13.—Tadâgi-Mudrâ.

61. Sitting in Paschimottana-posture, make the stomach like a tank (hollow). This is Tadâgî (Tank) Mudra, destroyer of decay and death.

14.—Mânduki-Mudrâ.

62. Closing the mouth, move the tip of the tongue towards the palate, and taste slowly the nectar (flowing from the Thousand-petalled Lotus.) This is Frog-mudrâ.

Its benefits.

63. The body never sickens or becomes old, and it retains perpetual youth ; the hair never grows white, of him who practises this.

15.—S'ÂMBHAVÎ-MUDRÂ.

64. Fixing the gaze between the two eye-brows, behold the self-existent. This is S'ambhavî, secret in all the Tantras.

Its benefits.

65. The Vedas, the scriptures, the Purâṇas are like public women, but this Sâmbhavî should be guarded as if it were a lady of a respectable family.

66. He, who knows this S'âmbhavî, is like the Âdinâtha, he is a Nârâyaṇa, he is Brahmâ the Creator.

67. Maheśwara has said "Truly, truly, and again truly, he who knows the S'ambhavî, is Brahma. There is no doubt in this."

THE FIVE DHÂRAṆÂ-MUDRÂS.

68. The S'âmbhavî has been explained; hear now the five Dhâraṇâs. Learning these five Dhâraṇâs what cannot be accomplished in this world ?

69. By this, with the human body one can visit and revisit Svarga-loka, he can go wherever he likes, as swiftly as mind, he acquires the faculty of walking in the sky. These five Dhâraṇâs are :—Pârthivi (earthy), Âmbhasi (Watery), Vâyavî (aerial), Âgneyî (Fiery), and Âkâsî (Etherial).

(*a*).—PÂRTHIVÎ.

70. The Prithivî-Tatva has the color of orpiment (yellow), the letter la (ल) is its secret symbol or seed (बीज), its form is four-sided, and Brahmâ is its presiding deity. Place this Tatva in the heart, and fix by Kumbhaka the Prâṇa-Vâyus and the Chitta there for the period of five ghatikas (2½ hours). This is called Adhodhâraṇa. By this, one conquers the Earth and no earthy-elements can injure him : and it causes steadiness.

Its benefits.

71. He who practises this dhâraṇâ, becomes like the conqueror of Death ; as an Adept he walks over this earth.

(*b*).—ÂMBHASÎ.

72. The Water-Tatva is white like the Kunda-flower or a conch or moon, its form is circular like the moon, the letter व (va) is the seed of this ambrosial element, and Vishṇu is its presiding deity. By yoga, produce the water-tatva in the heart, and fix there the Prâṇa with the Chitta (consciousness), for five ghatikas practising Kumbhaka. This is Watery Dharaṇâ ; it is the destroyer of all sorrows. Water cannot injure him who practises this.

Its benefits.

73—74. The Âmbhasî is a great mudrâ; the Yogî who knows it, never meets death even in the deepest water. This should be kept carefully concealed. By revealing it success is lost, verily I tell you the truth.

(*c*.)—ÂGNEYÎ.

75. The Fire-Tatva is situated at the navel, its colour is red like the Indra-gope insect, its form is triangular, its seed is ra, (र,) its presiding deity is Rudra. It is refulgent like the sun, and the giver of success. Fix the prâṇa along with the Chitta in this Tatva for five Ghatikas. This is called fire-dhâraṇâ, destroyer of the fear of dreadful death, and fire cannot injure him.

Its benefits.

76. If the practitioner is thrown into burning fire, by virtue of this Mudrâ he remains alive, without fear of death.

(*d.*)—VÂYAVÎ.

77. The Air-tatva is black as ungnent for the eyes, (collirium), the letter ya य is its seed, and Ísvara its presiding deity. This Tatva is full of Satva quality. Fix the prâṇa and the Chitta for five Ghatikas in this Tatva. This is Vâyavî Dhâraṇâ. By this the practitioner walks in the air.

Its benefits.

78—79. This great Mudrâ destroys decay and death. Its practitioner is never killed by any aerial disturbances; by its virtue one walks in the air. This should not be taught to the wicked or to those devoid of faith. By so doing success is lost; Oh Chandi! this is verily the truth.

(*e*).—ÂKÂŚÎ DHÂRAṆÂ.

80. The Ether-Tatva has the colour of pure sea-water, ह ha is its seed, its presiding deity is Sadâ-

śiva. Fix the Prâṇas along with Chitta for five Ghatikas in this Tatva. This is Ether-Dhâraṇâ. It opens the gates of emancipation.

Its benefits.

81. He who knows this Dhâraṇâ is the real Yogî. Death does not approach him, nor does he perish at the Pralaya.

21.—Aśvinî—mudrâ.

82. Contract and dilate the anal aperture again and again, this is called Aśvinî-mudrâ. It awakens the S'akti. (Kundalini).

Its benefits.

83. This aśvini is a great Mudrâ, it destroys all diseases of the rectum; it gives strength and vigour, and prevents premature death.

22.—Pâśinî—mudrâ.

84. Throw the two legs on the neck towards the back, holding them strongly together like a Pâśa (a noose). This is called Pâśinî-mudrâ ; it awakens the S'akti (Kundalinî.)

Its benefits.

85. This grand mudrâ gives strength and nourishment. It should be practised with care by those who desire success.

23.—Kâkî-mudrâ.

86. Contract the lips, like the beak of a crow, and drink (draw in) the air slowly and slowly. This is Kâkî (crow) mudrâ, destroyer of all diseases.

Its benefits.

87. The Kaki Mudrâ is a great Mudrâ, kept secret in all Tantras. By virtue of this, one becomes free from disease like a crow.

24.—Mâtangini-mudrâ.

88—89. Stand in neck-deep water, draw in the water through the nostrils, and throw it out by the mouth. Then draw in the water through [the mouth and expel it through] the nostrils. Let one repeat this again and again. This is called Elephant-mudrâ, destroyer of decay and death.

Its benefits.

90—91. In a solitary place, free from human intrusion, one should practise with fixed attention this Elephant mudrâ: by so doing he becomes strong like Elephant. Wherever he may be, by this process the Yogî enjoys great pleasure; therefore this mudrâ should be practised with great care.

25.—Bhujanginî-mudrâ.

92. Extending the neck a little forward, let him drink (draw in) air through the œsophagus; this is called Serpent-mudrâ, destroyer of decay and death.

Its benefits.

93. This Serpent-mudrâ quickly destroys all stomach diseases, especially indigestion, dispepsia &c.

THE BENEFITS OF MUDRÂS.

94. O Chanda-Kâpâla! thus have I recited to

thee the chapter on Mudrâs. This is beloved of all adepts, and destroys decay and death.

95. This should not be taught indiscriminately nor to a wicked person, nor to one devoid of faith ; this should be preserved secret with great care ; it is difficult to be attained even by the Devas.

96. These Mudrâs which give happiness and emancipation should be taught to a guileless, calm and peace-minded person who is devoted to his Teacher and comes of good family.

97. These Mudras destroy all diseases. They increase the gastric fire of him who practises them daily.

98. To him death never comes, nor decay &c.; there is no fear to him from fire and water, nor from air.

99. Cough, asthma, enlargement of spleen, leprosy, being diseases of twenty sorts, are verily destroyed by the practice of these Mudrâs.

100. O Chanda ! What more shall I tell thee ? In short, there is nothing in this world like the Mudrâs for giving quick success.

FOURTH LESSON.

PRATYÂHÂRA OR RESTRAINING THE MIND.

GHERANDA SAID :—1. Now I shall tell thee, Pratyâhâra-Yoga the best. By its knowledge, all the passions like lust, &c., are destroyed.

2. Let one bring the Chitta (thinking principle) under his control by withdrawing it, whenever it wanders away drawn by the various objects of sight.

3. Praise or censure : good speech or bad speech; let one withdraw his mind from all these and bring the Chitta under the control of the Self.

4. From sweet smells or bad smells, by whatever odour the mind may be distracted or attracted, let one withdraw the mind from that, and bring the thinking principle under the control of his Self.

5. From sweet or acid tastes, from bitter or astringent tastes, by whatever taste the mind may be attracted, let one withdraw it from that, and bring it within the control of his Self.

FIFTH LESSON.

PRÂṆÂYÂMA OR RESTRAINT OF BREATH.

GHERANDA SAID :—1. Now I shall tell thee the rules of Prâṇâyâma or regulation of breath. By its practice a man becomes like a god.

2. Four things are necessary in practising Prâṇâyâma. First, a good place; second, a suitable time, third moderate food, and lastly the purifications of the nâdis, (vessels of the body, *i.e.* alimentary canal, &c.)

Place.

3. The practice of Yoga should not be attempted in a far off country (from home), nor in a forest, nor in a capital city, nor in the midst of a crowd. If one does so, he loses success.

4. In a distant country, one loses faith (because of the Yoga not being known there); in a forest one is without protection; and in the midst of a thick population, there is danger of exposure (for then the curious will trouble him). Therefore let one avoid these three.

5. In a good country whose king is just, where food is easily and abundantly procurable, where there are no disturbances, let one erect there a small hut, around it let him raise walls.

6. And in the centre of the hut, let him sink a well and dig a tank. Let the hut be neither very high nor very low: let it be free from insects.

7. It should be completely plastered over with cow-dung. In a hut thus built and situated in such a hidden place, let him practise Prâṇâyâma.

Time.

8. The practise of Yoga should not be commenced in these four seasons out of six:—hemanta (winter), śiśira (cold), grîshma (hot), varshâ (rainy). If one begins in these seasons, he will contract diseases.

9. The practice of Yoga should be commenced by a beginner in spring (vasanta); and autumn (śarat). By so doing, he attains success; and verily he does not become liable to diseases.

10. The six seasons occur in their order in the twelve months beginning with Chaitra and ending with Phâlguna: two months being occupied by each season. But each season is experienced for four months beginning with Mâgha and ending with Phâlguna.

SIX SEASONS.

11. The six seasons are as follows :—

Season.	*Months Sanskrit.*	*English.*
Vasanta or Spring.	Chaitra and Vaiśâkha	March, April.
Grîshma or Summer.	Jeshtha and Asâdha	May, June.
Varshâ or Rainy.	S'râvaṇa and Bhâdra	July, August.
S'arat or Autumn.	Aśvina and Kârtika	Sept., Oct.
Hemanta or Winter.	Agrahâyaṇa and Pausha	Nov., Dec.
S'iśira or Cold.	Mâgha and Phálguna	January, February

The experiencing of seasons.

12—14. Now I shall tell thee the experiencing of seasons. They are as follows :—

Beginning from.	*Ending with*	*Season.*	*English.*
Mâgha	Vaiśâkha	Varshânubhava	January to April.
Chaitra	Ashâdha	Grîshmânubhâva	March to June.
Ashâdha	Aśvina	Varshânubhava	June to September.
Bhádra	Agrahâyaṇa	S'aradánubhava	August to Nov.
Kârtika	Mágha	Hemnátanubhava	Oct. to Jan.
Agrahayaṇa	Phálguna	S'iśiránubhava	Nov. to Feb.

15. The practice of Yoga should be commenced either in Vasanta (spring) or S'arat (autumn). For in these seasons success is attained without much trouble.

3.—*Moderation of diet.*

16. He who practises Yoga without moderation of diet, incurs various diseases, and obtains no success.

17. A Yogî should eat rice, barley (bread), or wheaten bread. He may eat Mudga beans मुग (Phaseolus Mungo), Mâsha bean (Phaseolus radiatus

Guz Arada, Hindi, Urada or उरिद,), gram &c. These should be clean white and free from chaff.

18—19. A Yogî may eat patola (a kind of cucumber, परवर), jack-fruit, mânakachu (Arum Colocasia), kakkola (a kind of berry), the jujube, the bonduc nut (Boorducella guilandina), cucumber, plantain, fig ; the unripe plantain, the small plantain, the plantain stem, and roots, brinjol, and medicinal roots and fruits (e. g. riddhi &c.)

20. He may eat green fresh vegetables बालशाक black vegetables (कालशाक), the leaves of patola, the Vâstûka-śâka, and hima-lochikâ S'âka. These are the five śákas (vegetable leaves) praised as fit food for Yogîs.

21. Pure, sweet and cooling food should be eaten to fill half the stomach : eating thus sweet juices with pleasure, and leaving the other half of the stomach empty is called moderation in diet.

22. Half the stomach should be filled with food, one quarter with water : and one quarter should be kept empty for practising práṇáyáma.

Prohibited foods.

23. In the beginning of Yoga-practice one should discard bitter, acid, salt, pungent and roasted things, curd, whey, heavy vegetables, wine, palmnuts, and over-ripe jack-fruit.

24. So also kulattha and masur beans, pandu fruit, pumpkins and vegetable stems, gourds, berries kutha-bel, (feronia elephantum), kaṇta-bilva and palâśa (Butea frondosa).

25. So also Kadamba (Navclea eadamba,) jambîral (citron), bimba, lukucha (a kind of bread fruit tree), onions, lotus, Kâmaranga, piyâla (Buchanânia latifolia), hinga (assafœtida), śálmali, kemuka. A beginner should avoid much travelling, company of women, and warming himself by fire.

26. So also he should avoid fresh butter, ghee, thickened milk, sugar, and date-sugar &c., as well as ripe plantain, cocoa-nut, pomegranate, dates, navanî fruit, âmlaki (myrabolans), and every thing containing acid juices.

27. But eardamom, jaiphal, cloves, uphrodisiacs or stimulants, the rose-apple, haritaki, and palm dates, a Yogî may eat while practising Yoga.

28. Easily digestible, agreeable and cooling foods which nourish the humours of the body, a Yogî may eat according to his desire.

29. But a Yogî should avoid hard (not easily digestible) sinful food, or putrid food, or very hot, or very stale food, as well as very cooling or very much exciting food.

30. He should avoid early (morning before sunrise) baths, fasting, &c., or anything giving pain to the body ; so also are prohibited to him eating only once a day, or not eating at all. But he may remain without food for 3 hours.

31. Regulating his life in this way let him practise Prâṇâyâma. In the beginning before commencing it, he should take a little milk and ghee daily, and

take his food twice daily, once at noon, and once in the evening.

4.—Purification of Nâdis.

32. He should sit on a seat of Kuśa-grass, or an antelope skin, or tiger skin, or a blanket, or on earth, calmly and quietly facing east or north. Having purified the nâdis, let him begin Prâṇâyâma.

Chandakâpâli said :—33. O ocean of mercy! How are nâdis purified, what is the purification of nâdis ; I want to learn all this ; recite this to me.

Gheranda said :—34. The Vâyu does not (cannot) enter the nâdis so long as they are full of impurities (*e. g.* fæces &c.). How then can Prâṇâyâma be accomplished? How can there be knowledge of Tatvas? Therefore first the Nâdis should be purified, and then Prâṇâyâma should be practised.

35. The purification of nâdis is of two sorts :— Samanuh and Nirmanuh. The Samanuh is done by a mental process with Bîja-mantra. The Nirmanuh is performed by physical cleanings.

36. The physical cleanings or Dhautis have aready been taught. They consist of the six Sadhanas. Now, O Chanda, listen to the Samanuh process of purifying the vessels.

37. Sitting in the Padmasana posture, and performing the adoration of the Guru &c., as taught by the Teacher, let him perform purification of Nadis for success in Práṇáyáma.

38—39. Contemplating on Vâyu-Bîja (*i. e.* यं), full of energy and of a smoke-colour, let him draw in breath by the left nostril repeating the Bîja sixteen times. This is Pûraka. Let him restrain the breath for a period of sixty-four repetitions of the Mantra. This is Kumbhaka. Then let him expel the air by the right nostril slowly during a period occupied by repeating the Mantra thirty-two times.

40—41. The root of the navel is the seat of Agni-Tatva. Raising the fire from that place, join the Prithivî-Tatva with it; then contemplate on this mixed light. Then repeating sixteen times the Agni-Bîja (रं), let him draw in breath by the right nostril, and retain it for the period of sixty-four repetitions of the Mantras, and then expel it by the left nostril for a period of thirty-two repetitions of the Mantra.

42—43. Then fixing the gaze on the tip of the nose and contemplating the luminous reflection of the moon there, let him inhale through the left nostril, repeating the Bija tham (ठं) sixteen times; let him retain it by repeating the Bîja (ठं) sixty-four times; in the meanwhile imagine (or contemplate) that the nectar flowing from the moon at the tip of the nose runs through all the vessels of the body, and purifies them. Thus contemplating, let him expel the air by repeating thirty-two times the Prithivî-Bîja lam (लं).

44. By these three Práṇáyámas the nâdîs are purified. Then sitting firmly in a posture, let him begin regular Práṇáyáma.

Kinds of Kumbhaka.

45. The Kumbhakas or retractions of breath are of eight sorts: Sahita, Sûrya-bheda, Ujjâyî, S'îtalî, Bhastrikâ, Bhrâmarî, Mûrchhâ and Kevalî.

1.—Sahita.

46. The Sahita Kumbhaka is of two sorts:—Sagarbha and Nirgarbha. The Kumbhaka performed by the repetition of Bîja Mantra is Sagarbha; that done without such repetition is Nirgarbha.

47. First I shall tell thee the Sagarbha Prâṇâyâma. Sitting in Sukhâsana posture, facing east or north, let him contemplate on Brahma full of Rajas quality of a blood-red colour, in the form of the letter अ.

48. Let the wise practitioner inhale by the left nostril repeating अं sixteen times. Then before he begins retention (but at the end of inhalation) let him perform Uddîyânabandha.

49. Then let him retain breath by repeating उ sixty-four times contemplating on Hari, of a black colour and of Satva quality.

50. Then let him exhale the breath through right nostril by repeating man (मँ) thirty-two times, contemplating S'iva of a white colour and of Tamas quality.

51. Then again inhale through Pingalâ (right nostril), retain by Kumbhaka, and exhale by Idâ (left), in the method taught above, changing the nostrils alternately.

52. Let him practise thus alternating the nostrils again and again. When inhalation is completed, close both nostrils, the right one by the thumb and the left one by the ring-finger and little-finger, never using the index and middle-fingers. The nostrils to be closed so long as Kumbhaka is.

53. The Nirgarbha (or simple or mantraless) Prâṇâyâma is performed without the repetition of Bîja mantra ; and the period of Pûraka (inhalation or inspiration), Kumbhaka (retention) and Rechaka (expiration), may be extended from one to hundred mâtrâs.

54. The best is twenty Mâtrâs : *i. e.* Pûraka 20 seconds, Kumbhaka 80, and Rechaka 40 seconds. The sixteen mâtrâs is middling *i. e.* 16,64 and 32. The twelve mâtrâs is the lowest *i. e.* 12,48,24. Thus the Prâṇâyâma is of three sorts.

55. By practising the lowest Prâṇâyâma for sometime, the body begins to perspire copiously ; by practising the middling, the body begins to quiver (especially there is a feeling of quivering along the spinal cord). By the highest Prâṇâyâma, one leaves the ground *i. e.* there is levitation. These signs attend the success of these three sorts of Prâṇâyâma.

56. By Prâṇâyâma is attained the power of levitation (Khecharî S'akti), by Prâṇâyâma diseases are cured, by Prâṇâyâma the S'akti (spiritual energy) is awakened, by Prâṇâyâma is obtained the calmness of mind and exaltation of mental powers

(clairvoyance &c.); by this, mind becomes full of bliss; verily the practitioner of Prâṇâyâma is happy.

2.—Sûryabheda Kumbhaka.

Gheranda said:—57—58. I have told thee, the Sahita Kumbhaka, now hear the Sûryabheda. Inspire with all your strength the external air through the sun-tube (right nostril): retain this air with the greatest care, performing the Jâlandhara Mudrâ. Let the Kumbhaka be kept up so long as the perspiaration does not burst out from the tips of the nails and the roots of the hair.

The Vâyus.

59. The Vâyus are ten, namely Prâṇa, Apâna, Samâna, Udâna and Vyâna; Nâga, Kúrma, Krikara, Devadatta and Dhananjaya.

Their Seats.

60—61. The Prâṇa moves always in the heart; the Apâna in the sphere of anus; the Samâna, in the navel region; the Udâna in the throat; and Vyâna pervades the whole body. These are the five principal Vâyus, known as Prâṇâdi. They belong to the Inner body. The Nâgâdi five Vâyus belong to the outer body.

62—63. I now tell thee the seats of these five external Vâyus. The Nâga-Vâyu performs the function of fructation; the Kûrma opens the eyelids, the Krikara causes sneezing; the Devadatta does yawning; the Dhananjaya pervades the whole gross body, and does not leave it even after death.

64. The Nâga-Vâyu gives rise to consciousness, the Kûrma causes vision, the Kṛikara hunger and thirst, the Devadatta produces yawning, and by Dhananjaya sound is produced; this does not leave the body ever.

65.—66. All these Vâyus, separated by the Sûrya-nâdî, let him raise up from the root of the navel; then let him expire by the Idâ-nâdî, slowly and with unbroken continuous force. Let him again draw the air through the right nostril, retaining it as taught above, and exhale it again. Let him do this again and again. In this process, the air is always inspired through the Sûrya-nâdî.

Its benefits.

67. The Sûrya-bheda Kumbhaka destroys decay and death, awakens the Kuṇdalî śakti, increases the bodily fire. O Chaṇda! thus have I taught thee the Sûryabhedana kumbhaka.

N.B.—The description of this process as given in Hatha-Yoga Pradîpikâ is somewhat different. Soon after Pûraka (inspiration), one should perform Jâlandhar and at the end of Kumbhaka but before Rechaka perform the Uddîyânabandha. Then quickly contract the anal orifice by Mûlabandha, contract the throat, pull in the stomach towards the back; by this process the air is forced into the Brahma-nâdî (Sushumṇâ). Raise the Apâna up, lower the Prâṇa below the Kaṇtha; a Yogî becomes free from decay: the air should be drawn through the right nostril and expelled through the left.

3.—Ujjâyî.

68. Close the mouth, draw in the external air by both the nostrils, and pull up the internal air from lungs and throat; retain them in the mouth.

69. Then having washed the mouth (*i.e.* expelled air through mouth) perform Jâlandhara. Let him perform Kumbhaka with all his might and retain the air unhindered.

70—71. All works are accomplished by Ujjâyî Kumbhaka. He is never attacked by Phlegm diseases, or nervous diseases, or indigestion, or dysentery, or consumption, or cough ; or fever or spleen. Let a man perform Ujjâyî to destroy decay and death.

N.B.—See the Hatha-Yoga Pradîpikâ Chap. II.—51, 53 for a different description of this.

4.—S'îtalî.

72. Draw in the air through the mouth (with the lips contracted and tongue thrown out), and fill the stomach slowly. Retain it there for a short time. Then exhale it through both the nostrils.

73. Let the Yogî always practise this S'îtalî Kumbhaka, giver of bliss ; by so doing he will be free from indigestion, phlegm and bilious disorders.

5.—Bhastrikâ (Bellow).

74. As the bellows of the ironsmith constantly dilate and contract, similarly let him slowly draw in the air by both the nostrils and expand the stomach ; then throw it out quickly, (the wind making sound like bellows).

75—76. Having thus inspired and expired quickly twenty times, let him perform Kumbhaka; then let him expel it by the previous method. Let the wise one perform this Bhastrikâ (bellows-like) Kumbhaka thrice : he will never suffer any disease and will be always healthy.

6.—BHRÂMARÎ (OR BEETLE-DRONING KUMBHAKA.)

77. At past midnight in a place where there are no sounds of any animals &c. to be heard, let the Yogî practise Pûraka and Kumbhaka, closing the ears by the hands.

78—79. He will hear then various internal sounds in his right ear. The first sound will be like that of crickets, then that of a lute, then that of a thunder, then that of a drum, then that of a beetle, then that of bells, then those of gongs of bell-metal, trumpets, kettle-drums, mridanga, military drums, and dundubhi, &c.

80—81. Thus various sounds are cognised by daily practice of this Kumbhaka. Last of all is heard the Anâhata sound rising from the heart ; of this sound there is a resonance, in that resonance there is a Light. In that Light the mind should be immersed. When mind is absorbed there it reaches the Highest seat of Vishṇu (parama pada) By success in this Bhrâmarî Kumbhaka one gets success in Samâdhi.

7.—MÛRCHHÂ.

82. Having performed Kumbhaka with comfort let him withdraw the mind from all objects and fix it in the space between the two eye-brows. This causes fainting of the mind, and gives happi-

ness. For, by thus joining the Manas with the Âtmâ, the bliss of Yoga is certainly obtained.

8.—Kevalî.

83. The breath of every person in entering makes the sound of "sah" and in coming out, that of "ham." These two sounds make सोऽहम् (so'ham "I am That,") or हंस: (Hamsa "The Great Swan"). Throughout a day and a night there are twenty-one thousand and six hundred such respirations, (that is 15 respirations per minute). Every living being (Jîva) performs this japa unconsciously, but constantly. This is called Ajapâ gáyatrî.

84. This Ajapâ japa is performed in three places *i. e.* in the Mûládhâra (the space between anus and membrum virile), in the Anâhat lotus (heart), and in Âjnya lotus (the space where the two nostrils join).

85.—86. This body of Vâyu is ninety-six digits length (*i. e.* six feet) as a standard. The ordinary length of the air-current when expired is twelve digits (nine inches); in singing, its length becomes sixteen digits (one foot); in eating, it is twenty digits (15 inches); in walking it is twenty-four digits (18 inches); in sleep it is thirty digits (27½ inches); in copulation it is thirty-six digits (27 inches), and in taking physical exercise it is more than that.

87. By decreasing the natural length of the expired current from nine inches to less and less,

there takes place increase of life; and by increasing the current, there is decrease of life.

88. So long as breath remains in the body there is no death. When the full length of the wind is all confined in the body, nothing being allowed to go out, it is Kevala Kumbhaka.

89.—90. All Jîvas are constantly and unconsciously reciting this Ajapâ Mantra, only for a fixed number of times every day. But a Yogî should recite this consciously and counting the numbers. By doubling the number of Ajapâ (*i.e.* by 30 respirations per minute), the state of Manonmanî (fixedness of mind) is attained. There are no regular Rechaka and Pûraka in this process. It is only (Kevala) Kumbhaka.

91. By inspiring air by both nostrils let him perform Kevala Kumbhaka. On the first day let him retain breath from one to sixty-four times.

92.—93. This Kevalî should be performed eight times a day, once in every three hours; or one may do it five times a day, as I shall tell thee. First in the early morning, then at noon, then in the twilight, then at mid-night, and then in the fourth quarter of the night. Or one may do it thrice a day *i. e.* in the morning, noon and evening.

94.—95. So long as success is not obtained in Kevalî, he should increase the length of Ajapâ japa every day one to five times. He who knows Prâṇâyâma and Kevalî is the real Yogî. What can he not accomplish in this world who has acquired success in Kevalî Kumbhaka?

SIXTH LESSON.

Dhyâna-Yoga.

Gherand said:—1. The Dhyána or contemplation is of three sorts: gross, subtle and luminous. When a particular figure such as one's Guru or Deity is contemplated, it is Sthûla or gross contemplation. When Brahma or Prakriti is contemplated as a mass of light, it is called Jyotis contemplation. When Brahma as a Bindu (point) and Kundalí force are contemplated, it is Sûkshma or Subtle contemplation.

1.—Sthûla Dhyâna:

2.—8. Having closed the eyes, let him contemplate that there is a sea of nectar in his heart: that in the midst of that sea there is an island of precious stones, the very sand of which is pulverised diamonds and rubies. That on all sides of it, there are Kadamba trees, laden with sweet flowers; that, next to these trees, like a rampart there is a row of flowering trees such as mâlati, malliká, játí, kesara, champaka, párijáta and padmas, and that the fragrance of these flowers is spread all round in every quarter. In the middle of this garden, let the Yogî imagine that there stands a beautiful Kalpa tree, having four branches, representing the four Vedas, and that it is full of flowers and fruits. Insects are humming there and kuckoos singing. Beneath that tree let him imagine a rich platform of precious gems, and on that a costly throne inlaid with jewels, and that on that throne sits his particular Deity, as taught to him by his Guru.

Let him contemplate on the appropriate form, ornaments and vehicle of that Deity. The constant contemplation of such a form is 'Sthûla Dhyâna.

Another process.

9.—11. Let the Yogî imagine that in the pericarp of the great thousand-petalled Lotus (Brain) there is a smaller lotus having twelve petals. Its colour is white, highly luminous, having twelve bíja letters, named ह, स, क्ष, म, ल, व, र, युँ, ह, स, ख, फ्रें, (ha sa ksha ma la va ra yum ha sa kha phrem). In the pericarp of this smaller lotus there are three lines forming a triangle अ, क, थ (a ka tha): having three angles called ह, ल, क्ष (ha la ksha): and in the middle of this triangle there is the Praṇava ओम्—Om.

12. Then let him contemplate that in that there is a beautiful seat having Nâda and Bindu. On that seat there are two swans, and a pair of wooden sandals or shoes.

13.—14. There let him contemplate his Guru Deva, having two arms and two eyes, and dressed in pure white, anointed with white sandal-paste, wearing garlands of white flowers; to the left of whom stands S'akti of blood-red colour. By thus contemplating the Guru, the Sthûla Dhyána is attained.

2.—Jyotir Dhyâna.

15. I have told thee the Sthûla Dhyâna; listen now to the contemplation of Light, by which the Yogî attains success and sees his Self.

10. In the Mûlâdhâra is kuṇdalini, having the form of a serpent. The Jivâtmâ is there like the flame of a lamp. Contemplate on this flame as the Luminous Brahma. This is the Tejo Dhyâna or Jyotir Dhyâna.

Another process.

17. In the middle of the two eye-brows, above the Manas, there is a Light consisting of Om. Let him contemplate on this flame. This is another method of contemplation of Light.

3.—Sûkshma Dhyâna.

Gheranda said—18.—19. O Chaṇda! thou hast heard the Tejo Dhyâna, listen now to the Sûkshma Dhyâna. When by a great good fortune, the Kuṇdalí is awakened, it joins with the Âtmâ and leaves the body through the portals of the two eyes; and enjoys itself by walking in the royal road (Astral Light). It cannot be seen on account of its subtleness and great changeability.

20. The Yogî however attains this success by performing S'ámbhaví Mudrá *i.e.* by gazing fixedly at space without winking. (Then he will see his Sûkshma S'arira). This is called Sûkshma Dhyána, difficult to be attained even by the Devas, as it is a great mystery.

21. The contemplation of Light is a hundred times superior to contemplation of Form; and a hundred thousand times superior to Tejo Dhyána is the contemplation of the Sûkshma.

22. O Chanda! thus have I told thee the Dhyána Yoga—a most precions knowledge; for, by it there is direct perception of the Self. Hence Dhyána is belauded.

SEVENTH LESSON.

SAMÂDHI YOGA.

Gheranda said—1. The Samádhi is a great Yoga; it is acqnired by great good fortune. It is obtained throngh the grace and kindness of the Gurn, and by intense devotion to him.

2. That Yogî quickly attains this most beautiful practice of Samádhi, who has confidence (or faith) in knowledge, faith in his own Guru, faith in his own Self; and whose mind (manas) awakens to intelligence from day to day.

3. Separate the Manas from the body, and unite it with the Paramátmá. This is known as Samádhi or Mukti from all states of consciousness.

4. I am Brahma, I am nothing else, the Brahma is certainly I, I am not participator of sorrow, I am Existence, Intelligence and Bliss; always free, of one essence.

5—6. The Samádhi is four-fold i.e. Dhyána-Samádhi, Náda-Samádhi, Rasánand-Samâdhi, and Laya-Samádhi: respectively accomplished by S'ambhaví Mndrá, Khechari Mudrá, Bhrámarí Mudrá and Yoni-Mudrá. The Bhakti-Yoga Samádhi is fifth, and Rája-Yoga Samâdhi attained through Mano-Mûrchhá Kumbhaka, is the sixth form of Samádhi.

1.—Dhyâna-Yoga Samâdhi.

7. Peforming the S'ámbhavi Mudrâ, perceive the Âtmâ. Having seen once the Brahma in a Bindu (point of light), fix the mind in that point.

8. Bring the Âtmâ in Kha (Ether), bring the Kha (Ether or Space) in the Âtmâ. Thus seeing the Âtmâ full of Kha (Space or Brahma), nothing will obstruct him. Being full of perpetual bliss, the man enters Samádhi (Trance or Ecstasy).

2.—Nâda-Yoga Samâdhi.

9. Turn the tongue upwards closing the wind-passages, by performing the Khechari Mudrá ; by so doing Samádhi (trance asphyxiation) will be induced; there is no necessity of performing anything else.

3.—Rasânanda Yoga Samâdhi.

10—11. Let him perform the Bhrámarí Kumbhaka drawing in the air slowly : expel the air slowly and slowly, with a buzzing sound like that of beetle Let him carry the Manas and place it in the centre of this sound of humming beetle. By so doing there will be Samádhi and by this, knowledge of 'so' ham' (I am That) arises and a great happiness takes place.

4.—Laya-Siddhi Yoga Samâdhi.

12.—13. Perform the Yonî-Mudrá, and let him imagine that he is S'akti, and Paramátmá is Purusha;

and that both have been united in one. By this he becomes full of bliss, and realises Aham Brahma, 'I am Brahma.' This conduces to Advaita Samádhi.

5.—Bhakti Yoga Samâdhi.

14—15. Let him contemplate within his heart his special Diety ; let him be full of ecstasy by such contemplation, let him shed tears of happiness and by so doing he will become entranced. This leads to Samádhi and Manonmaní.

6.—Râja-Yoga Samâdhi.

16. Performing Manomúrchhá Kumbhaka, unite the Manas with the Âtmâ. By this Union is obtained Rája-Yoga Samádhi.

7.—Praise of Samâdhi.

17. O Chaṇḍa! thus have I told thee about Samâdhi which leads to emancipation. Râja-Yoga Samádhi, Unmanî, Sahajávasthá are all synonyms, and mean the Union of Manas with Âtmâ.

18. Vishṇu is in water, Vishṇu is in earth, Vishṇu is on the peak of the mountain ; Vishṇu is in the midst of Volcanic fires and flames : the whole Universe is full of Vishṇu.

19. All these that walk on land or move in the air, all living and animate creation, trees, shrubs, roots, creepers and grass, &c., oceans and mountains —all, know ye, to be Brahma. See them all in Âtmâ.

20. The Âtmâ confined in the body is Chaitanya or Consciousness, it is without a second, the Eternal, the Highest; knowing it separate from body, let him be free from desires and passion.

21. Thus is Samádhi obtained, free from all desires. Free from attachment to his own body, to son, wife, friends, kinsmen, or riches; being free from all, let him obtain fully the Samâdhi.

22. S'iva has revealed many Tatvas, such as Laya Amrita, &c.; of them, I have told thee an abstract, leading to emancipation.

23. O Chaṇda ! thus have I told thee of Samâdhi difficult of attainment. By knowing this, there is no rebirth in this Sphere.

FINIS.

हठयोगान्तर्गता

घेरण्डसंहिता

श्रीसचन्द्रवसूनामभिः बीए, एफ्. टी. एस.

इत्युपपदधारिभिः शिवसंहितापाणिन्यादि-

ग्रन्थानां भाषान्तरकारिभिः विरचितैं-

ग्लिशभाषान्तरसहिता.

सा च

रा.रा. तुकारामतात्यां इत्येतैः एफ्.टी.एस्.

इत्युपपदधारिभिः

थिआसोफिकलपब्लिकेशनसमाजार्थं

मुम्बय्यां

"तत्त्वविवेचकाख्य" मुद्रणालये मुद्रयित्वा प्रसिद्धिं नीता.

इसवी सनः १८९५.

अस्य ग्रन्थस्य सर्वे अधिकाराः १८६७ तमस्य इसवी सनस्य
२५ तमराजनियमानुसारेण स्वायत्तीकृताः ।

प्रस्तावना.

भोभो विद्याधना महाजनाः, विदितमेवात्रभवतां भवतां वेदवेदाङ्गानुभवतां, यत् योगशास्त्रमखिलमहीतले वरिवर्तीति। यतो योगं पुरस्कृत्य महर्षिभिः खेचर्यादिमुद्रासाधनेन रवि-चन्द्रादीनां गत्यादिकमप्रत्यक्षमपि साक्षात्कृत्य सकलजनानुग्र-हकरणवाञ्छया ग्रन्थरूपेण सुधारस इव प्रसिद्धिमनीयत। वाग्भट्टाद्यैरपि योगमेव प्रसाध्य शारिरिकी स्थितिर्निरणायि इति अनुमीयते। कथमन्यथा तत्तत्स्थानरचनाः, वातपित्तश्लेष्मणां न्यूनाधिक्येन प्रादुर्भवन्तो रोगाः, तत्परिहाराश्च पराग्भिरि-न्द्रियैरयोगिभिर्ज्ञातुं शक्यन्ते। एवंरीत्या विचार्यमाणे ताप-त्रयोन्मूलने योगशास्त्रमेव शक्तमिति तावन्निर्विवादम्। तत्रात्र महति महनीये शास्त्रे प्रतिपिपादयिषया अनेके महर्षयः प्रयतिरे ग्रन्थांश्च निर्ममिरे। यान् पण्डितवराः पुष्पस्रजमिव शिरसाभिनन्दन्ति। तदेतद्योगशास्त्रमतिदुरधिगममपि सुगमं चिकीर्षन् परमकारुणिकस्तत्रभवान् तापसो घेरण्डश्चण्डकपा-लये घटस्थयोगं प्रणीतवान्। सेयं घेरण्डसंहिता योग-योगाङ्गज्ञाने अतीवोपकरोतीति यावद्वर्णयामस्तावत्स्वल्पमेव। इयं (घेरण्डसंहिता) कलिकातानगरे पूर्वं मुद्रितापि तद्गत-पाठानामशुद्धत्वं वर्णानां च दुरवगाहत्वं पर्यालोच्य पुस्त-कान्तराणि च महता कष्टेन संपाद्य यावच्छक्यं सम्यक् शोध-यित्वा पाठान्तराणि संगृह्य मुद्रापिता। तदेतत्सकलं मन-सिकृत्य ईदृशे कर्मणि प्रवृत्तस्य मम प्रयासः सफलः कार्य इति मुहुर्मुहुराशासे।

तुकाराम तात्या.

श्री गुरुदेवैर्हठयोगस्य सत्यतां, ऐक्यं, ततः समुत्पद्यमा-
नानि फलानि सुमहान्ति अनुभवैकगम्योदाहरण-
दानेन चोपदिश्येमं दुर्बोधं विषयं अहं
पाठित इति हठयोगस्येदं भाषान्तरं
महतादरेण प्रेम्णा च तान्प्रति
समर्पयामि तेषां नम्रः
सेवकः
भाषान्तरकर्ता.

सूचीपत्रम्.

घेरण्डसंहिता ।

प्रथमोपदेशः ।

घटस्थयोगकथनम् ।

आदीश्वराय प्रणमामि तस्मै
येनोपदिष्टा हठयोगविद्या ।
विराजते प्रोन्नतराजयोग-
मारोढुमिच्छोरधिरोहिणीव ॥

एकदा चण्डकापालिर्गत्वा घेरण्डकुट्टिमम्[1] ।
प्रणम्य विनयाद्भक्त्या घेरण्डं परिपृच्छति ॥ १ ॥

श्रीचण्डकापालि[2]रुवाच—

घटस्थयोगं योगेश तत्वज्ञानस्य कारणम् ।
इदानीं श्रोतुमिच्छामि योगेश्वर वद प्रभो ॥ २ ॥

घेरण्ड उवाच—

साधु साधु महाबाहो यन्मान्त्वं परिपृच्छसि ।
कथयामि हि ते वत्स सावधानोवधारय ॥ ३ ॥

नास्ति मायासमः पाशो नास्ति योगात्परं बलम् ।
नास्तिज्ञानात्परो बन्धुर्नाहङ्कारात् परो रिपुः ॥ ४ ॥

अभ्यासात्कादिवर्णानां यथा शास्त्राणि बोधयेत् ।
तथा योगं समासाद्य तत्त्वज्ञानञ्च लभ्यते ॥ ५ ॥

---

१ र. २ क.

सुकृतैर्दुष्कृतैः कार्यैर्जायते प्राणिनां घटः ।
घटादुत्पद्यते कर्म्म घटियन्त्रं यथा भ्रमेत् ॥ ६ ॥
उर्ध्वाधो भ्रमते यद्वद्घटियन्त्रं गवां वशात् ।
तद्वत्कर्म्मवशाज्जीवो भ्रमते जन्ममृत्युभिः ॥ ७ ॥
आमकुम्भ इवाम्भस्थो जीर्यमाणः सदा घटः ।
योगानलेन संदह्य घटशुद्धिं समाचरेत् ॥ ८ ॥

अथ सप्तसाधनम् ।

शोधनं दृढता चैव स्थैर्य्यं धैर्य्यञ्च लाघवम् ।
प्रत्यक्षञ्च निर्लिप्तञ्च घटस्य सप्तसाधनम् ॥ ९ ॥

अथ सप्तसाधनलक्षणम् ।

षट्कर्मणां शोधनञ्च आसनेन भवेद्दृढम् ।
मुद्रया स्थिरता चैव प्रत्याहारेण धीरता ॥ १० ॥
प्राणायामाल्लाघवञ्च ध्यानात्प्रत्यक्षमात्मनः ।
समाधिना निर्लिप्तञ्च मुक्तिरेव न संशयः ॥ ११ ॥

अथ शोधनम् ।

धौतिर्वस्तिस्तथा नेतिर्लौलिकी त्राठकं तथा ।
कपालभातिश्चैतानि षट्कर्म्माणि समाचरेत् ॥ १२ ॥

अथ धौतिः ।

अन्तर्धौतिर्दन्तधौतिर्हृद्धौतिर्मूलशोधनम् ।
धौतिं चतुर्विधां कृत्वा घटं कुर्वन्तु निर्मलम् ॥ १३ ॥

---

१ टी. २ स्थं. ३ षटकर्म. ४ नि. ५ लि. ६ तीं. ७ ती. ८ तीं.

अथ अन्तर्धौतिः।

वातसारं वारिसारं वह्निसारं बहिष्कृतम्।
घटस्य निर्म्मलार्थाय अन्तर्धौतिश्चतुर्विधा ॥ १४ ॥

अथ वातसारः।

काकचञ्चूवदास्येन[1] पिबेद्वायुं शनैः शनैः।
चालयेदुदरं पश्चाद्वर्त्मना रेचयेच्छनैः ॥ १५ ॥
वातसारं परं गोप्यं देहनिर्म्मलकारणम्।
सर्वरोगक्षयकरं देहानलविवर्द्धकम् ॥ १६ ॥

अथ वारिसारः।

आकण्ठं पूरयेद्वारि वक्त्रेण च पिबेच्छनैः।
चालयेदर्धवर्त्मेन[2] चोदराद्रेचयेदधः ॥ १७ ॥
वारिसारं परं गोप्यं देहनिर्म्मलकारकम्।
साधयेत्तत्प्रयत्नेन देवदेहं प्रपद्यते ॥ १८ ॥
वारिसारं परां[3] धौतिं[4] साधयेद्यः प्रयत्नतः।
मलदेहं शोधयित्वा देवदेहं प्रपद्यते ॥ १९ ॥

अथ अग्निसारः।

नाभिग्रन्थिं मेरुपृष्ठे[5] शतवारञ्च कारयेत्।
अग्निसारमेषा धौतिर्योगिनां योगसिद्धिदा।
उदरामयं संत्यक्त्वा जठराग्निं विवर्धयेत् ॥ २० ॥
एषा धौतिः परा गोप्या देवानामपि दुर्लभा।
केवलं धौतिमात्रेण देवदेहो भवेद्ध्रुवम् ॥ २१ ॥

---

१ ञ्चु. २ अकारान्तताऽऽर्षी वर्त्म शब्दे. ३ रं. ४ तं. ५ ष्ठं.

अथ वहिष्कृतधौतिः ।

काकीमुद्रां साधयित्वा पूरयेदुदरे मरुत् ।
धारयेदर्द्धयामन्तु चालयेदर्धवर्त्मना ।
एषा धौतिः परा गोप्या न प्रकाश्या कदाचन ॥२२॥

अथ प्रक्षालनम् ।

नाभिमग्नो[1] जले स्थित्वा शक्तिनाडीं विसर्जयेत् ।
कराभ्यां क्षालयेन्नाडीं यावन्मलविसर्जनम् ।
तावत्प्रक्षाल्य नाडीञ्च उदरे वेशयेत् पुनः ॥२३॥
इदं प्रक्षालनं गोप्यं देवानामपि दुर्लभम् ।
केवलं धौतिमात्रेण देवदेहो भवेद्ध्रुवम् ॥ २४ ॥

अथ बहिष्कृतधौतिप्रयोगः ।

यामार्धं धारणां शक्तिं यावन्न साधयेन्नरः ।
वहिष्कृतं महद्धौतिस्तावच्चैवं न जायते[2] ॥ २५ ॥

अथ दन्तधौतिः ।

दन्तमूलं जिह्वामूलं रन्ध्रञ्च कर्णयुग्मयोः ।
कपालरन्ध्रं पञ्चैते दन्तधौतिं विधीयते[3] ॥ २६ ॥

अथ दन्तमूलधौतिः ।

खादिरेण रसेनाथ मृत्तिकया च शुद्धया ।
मार्जयेद्दन्तमूलञ्च यावत्किल्बिषमाहरेत् ॥ २७ ॥
दन्तमूलं परां धौतिर्योगिनां योगसाधने ।
नित्यं कुर्य्यात्प्रभाते च दन्तरक्षां च योगवित् ।
दन्तमूलं धावनादिकार्य्येषु योगिनां मतम् ॥ २८ ॥

---

१ लग्न. २ नैवसमाचरेत्. ३ प्रचक्षते. ४ रं. ५ तं. ६ यतः.

अथ जिह्वाशोधनम् ।

अथातः संप्रवक्ष्यामि जिह्वाशोधनकारणम् ।
जरामरणरोगादीन्[1]नाशयेद्दीर्घलम्बिका ॥ २९ ॥

अथ जिह्वामूलधौतिप्रयोगः ।

तर्जनीमध्यमानामो[2] अङ्गुलित्रययोगतः ।
वेशयेद्गलमध्ये तु मार्जयेल्लम्बिकाम[3]लम् ।
शनैः शनैर्मार्जयित्वा कफदोषं निवारयेत् ॥ ३० ॥
मार्जयेन्नवनीतेन दोहयेच्च पुनः पुनः ।
तदग्रं लौहयन्त्रेण कर्षयित्वा शनैः शनैः ॥ ३१ ॥
नित्यं कुर्य्यात्प्रयत्नेन रवेरुदयकेऽस्तके ।
एवं कृते च नित्यं सा लम्बिका दीर्घतां व्रजेत् ॥३२॥

अथ कर्णधौतिप्रयोगः ।

तर्[4]जन्यनामिकायोर्गान्मार्जयेत् कर्णरन्ध्रयोः ।
नित्यमभ्यासयोगेन नादान्तरं प्रकाशयेत् ॥ ३३ ॥

अथ कपालरन्ध्रप्रयोगः ।

वृद्धाङ्गुष्ठेन दक्षेण मार्जयेद्भालरन्ध्रकम् ।
एवमभ्यासयोगेन कफदोषं[5] निवारयेत् ॥ ३४ ॥
नाडी निर्मलतां याति दिव्यदृष्टिः प्रजायते ।
निद्रान्ते भोजनान्ते च दिवा[6]न्ते च दिने दिने ॥३५॥

---

१ दि. २ मी. ३ मु. ४ तर्जन्यङ्गुलिनाङ्गुष्ठे । अयंच अशुद्धः पाठः. ५ रोगं. ६ एवं कुर्यात्.

अथ हृद्धौतिः।

हृद्धौतिं त्रिविधां कुर्य्याद्दण्डवमनवाससा ॥ ३६ ॥

अथ दण्डधौतिः।

रम्भादण्डं हरिद्रादण्डं वेत्रदण्डं तथैव च।
हृन्मध्ये चालयित्वा तु पुनः प्रत्याहरेच्छनैः ॥ ३७ ॥
कफपित्तं तथा क्लेदं रेचयेदूर्ध्ववर्त्मना।
दण्डधौतिविधानेन हृद्रोगं नाशयेद्ध्रुवम् ॥ ३८ ॥

अथ वमनधौतिः।

भोजनान्ते पिबेद्वारि चाकण्ठपूरितं सुधीः।
उर्ध्वां दृष्टिं क्षणं कृत्वा तज्जलं वमयेत्पुनः।
नित्यमभ्यासयोगेन कफपित्तं निवारयेत् ॥ ३९ ॥

अथ वासोधौतिः।

चतुरङ्गुलविस्तारं सूक्ष्मवस्त्रं शनैर्ग्रसेत्।
पुनः प्रत्याहरेदेतत्प्रोच्यते धौतिकर्म्मकम् ॥ ४० ॥
गुल्मज्वरप्लीहाकुष्ठकफपित्तं विनश्यति।
आरोग्यं बलपुष्टिश्च भवेत्तस्य दिने दिने ॥ ४१ ॥

अथ मूलशोधनम्।

अपानक्रूरता तावद्यावन्मूलं न शोधयेत्।
तस्मात्सर्वप्रयत्नेन मूलशोधनमाचरेत् ॥ ४२ ॥
पित्तमूलस्य दण्डेन मध्यमाङ्गुलिनापि वा।
यत्नेन क्षालयेद्गुह्यं वारिणा च पुनः पुनः ॥ ४३ ॥

---

१ हरिद्दण्डं. २ उर्ध्वं. ३ योगायं. ४ वित्. ५ पीत.

वारयेत्कोष्ठकाठिन्[1]यमामं[2]जीर्णं निवारयेत् ।
कारणं कान्तिपुष्ट्योश्च वह्निमण्डल दीपनम् ॥ ४४ ॥

अथ वस्तिप्रकरणम् ।

जलबस्तिः शुष्कबस्तिर्बस्तिः स्याद्द्विविधा स्मृता ।
जलबस्तिं जले कुर्याच्छुष्कबस्तिं सदा क्षितौ ॥ ४५ ॥

अथ जलबस्तिः ।

नाभिमग्नं[3]जले पायुं न्यस्तवानुत्कटासनम् ।
आकुञ्चनं प्रसारञ्च जलबस्तिं समाचरेत् ॥ ४६ ॥
प्रमेहञ्च गुदावर्त्तं क्रूरवायुं निवारयेत् ।
भवेत्स्वच्छन्ददेहश्च कामदेवसमो भवेत् ॥ ४७ ॥
बस्तिं पश्चिमतानेन चाँलयित्वा शनैरधः ।
अश्विनीमुद्रया पायुमाकुञ्चयेत् प्रसाँरयेत् ॥ ४८ ॥
एवमभ्यासयोगेन कोष्ठदोषो न विद्यते ।
विवर्द्धयेज्जठराग्निमामवातं विनाशयेत् ॥ ४९ ॥

अथ नेतियोगः ।

वितस्तिमानं सूक्ष्मसूत्रं नासानाले प्रवेशयेत् ।
मुखान्निर्गमयेत्पश्चात् प्रोच्यते नेतिकर्मकम् ॥ ५० ॥
साधनान्नेतिकार्यस्य खेचरीसिद्धिमाप्नुयात् ।
कफदोषा विनश्यन्ति दिव्यदृष्टिः प्रजायते ॥ ५१ ॥

---

१ न्यं. २ सा. ३ लग्न. ४ क्षा. ५ काश. ६ कुष्ठ. ७ मात्रं.
८ वत्रं ९ धौतकर्मवित+योगकर्मवित्.

अथ लौलिकीयोगः।

अमन्दवेगेन तुन्दं तु भ्रामयेदुभपार्श्वयोः।
सर्वरोगान्निहन्तीह देहानलविवर्द्धनम् ॥ ५२ ॥

अथ त्राटकम्।

निमेषोन्मेषकं त्यक्त्वा सूक्ष्मलक्ष्यं निरीक्षयेत्।
यावदश्रूणि पतन्ति त्राटकं प्रोच्यते बुधैः ॥ ५३ ॥
एवमभ्यासयोगेन शाम्भवी जायते ध्रुवम्।
नेत्ररोगा विनश्यन्ति दिव्यदृष्टिः प्रजायते ॥ ५४ ॥

अथ कपालभातिः।

वातक्रमेण व्युत्क्रमेण शीत्क्रमेण विशेषतः।
भालभातिं त्रिधा कुर्यात्कफदोषं निवारयेत् ॥ ५५ ॥

अथ वातक्रमकपालभातिः।

इडया पूरयेद्वायुं रेचयेत्पिङ्गलाक्षया।
पिङ्गलया पूरयित्वा पुनश्चन्द्रेण रेचयेत् ॥ ५६ ॥
पूरकं रेचकं कृत्वा वेगेन न तु चालयेत्।
एवमभ्यासयोगेन कफदोषं निवारयेत् ॥ ५७ ॥

अथ व्युत्क्रमकपालभातिः।

नासाभ्यां जलमाकृष्य पुनर्वक्त्रेण रेचयेत्।
पायं पायं व्युत्क्रमेण श्लेष्मदोषं निवारयेत् ॥ ५८ ॥

---

१ भ्रमेदुभय. २ निमेलोन्मेलनं. ३ श्रु निपतति. ४ णो. ५ इ. ६ पिङ्गया पुनः. ७ धारयेत्. ८ प्रकुर्वीत.

अथ शीत्क्रमकपालभातिः ।

शीत्कृत्य पीत्वा वक्त्रेण नासानालैर्विरेचयेत् ।
एवमभ्यासयोगेन कामदेवसमो भवेत् ॥ ५९ ॥
भवेत्स्वच्छन्ददेहश्च कफदोषं निवारयेत् ।
न जायते वार्द्धकं च ज्वरो नैव प्रजायते ॥ ६० ॥

इति श्रीघेरण्डसंहितायां घटस्थयोगे घेरण्डचण्ड-संवादे षट्कर्म्मसाधनं नाम प्रथमोपदेशः समाप्तः ।

द्वितीयोपदेशः ।

अथ आसनानि ।

घेरण्ड उवाच—

आसनानि समस्तानि यावन्तो जीवजन्तवः ।
चतुरशीतिलक्षाणि शिवेन कथितानि तु ॥ १ ॥
तेषां मध्ये विशिष्टानि षोडशोनं शतं कृतम् ।
तेषां मध्ये मर्त्यलोके द्वात्रिंशदासनं शुभम् ॥ २ ॥

अथ आसनानां भेदाः ।

सिद्धं पद्मं तथा भद्रं मुक्तं वज्रञ्च स्वस्तिकम् ।
सिंहञ्च गोमुखं वीरं धनुरासनमेव च ॥ ३ ॥

मृतं गुप्तं तथा मात्स्यं मत्स्येन्द्रासनमेव च ।
गोरक्षं पश्चिमोत्तानं उत्कटं सङ्कटं तथा ॥ ४ ॥
मायूरं कुक्कुटं कूर्म्मं तथा चोत्तानकूर्म्मकम् ।
उत्तानमण्डुकं वृक्षं मण्डुकं गरुडं वृषम् ॥ ५ ॥
शलभं मकरं चोष्ट्रं भुजङ्गञ्च योगासनम् ।
द्वात्रिंशदासनी प्रोक्ता मर्त्त्यलोके तु सिद्धिदा ॥ ६ ॥

अथ आसनानां प्रयोगाः

अथ सिद्धासनम् ।

योनिस्थानकमङ्घ्रिमूलघटितं संपीड्य गुल्फेतरं
मेढ्रोपर्यथ संनिधाय चिबुकं कृत्वा हृदि स्थापितम् ।
स्थाणुः संयमितेन्द्रियोऽचलदृशा पश्यन् भ्रुवोरन्तर-
मेतन्मोक्षकपाटभेदनकरं सिद्धासनं प्रोच्यते ॥ ७ ॥

अथ पद्मासनम् ॥

वामोरूपरि दक्षिणं हि चरणं संस्थाप्य वामं तथा
दक्षोरूपरि पश्चिमेन विधिना कृत्वा कराभ्यां दृढम् ।
अङ्गुष्ठौ हृदये निधाय चिबुकं नासाग्रमालोकये-
देतद्व्याधिविनाशनाशनकरं पद्मासनं प्रोच्यते ॥ ८ ॥

अथ भद्रासनम् ।

गुल्फौ च वृषणस्याधो व्युत्क्रमेण समाहितः ।
पादाङ्गुष्ठौ कराभ्याञ्च धृत्वा च पृष्ठदेशतः ॥ ९ ॥

---

१ यु. २ धृत्वा.

जालन्धरं समासाद्य नासाग्रमवलोकयेत्।
भद्रासनं भवेदेतत्सर्वव्याधिविनाशकम्॥ १० ॥

अथ मुक्तासनम्।

पायुमूले वामगुल्फं दक्षगुल्फं तथोपरि।
समकायशिरोग्रीवं मुक्तासनन्तु सिद्धिदम्॥ ११ ॥

अथ वज्रासनम्।

जङ्घाभ्यां वज्रवत्कृत्वा गुदपार्श्वे पदावुभौ।
वज्रासनं भवेदेतद्योगिनां सिद्धिदायकम्[1]॥ १२ ॥

अथ स्वस्तिकासनम्।

जानूर्वोरन्तरे कृत्वा योगी पादतले उभे।
ऋजुकायः समासीनः स्वस्तिकं तत्प्रचक्षते॥ १३ ॥

अथ सिंहासनम्।

गुल्फौ च वृषणस्याधो व्युत्क्रमेणोर्ध्वतां गतौ।
चितिमूलौ भूमिसंस्थौ कृत्वा[2] च जानुनोपरि॥ १४ ॥
व्यक्तवक्त्रो जलध्रं[3] च नासाग्रमवलोकयेत्।
सिंहासनं भवेदेतत् सर्वव्याधिविनाशकम्॥ १५ ॥

अथ गोमुखासनम्।

पादौ च भूमौ संस्थाप्य पृष्ठपार्श्वे निवेशयेत्।
स्थिरकायं समासाद्य गोमुखं गोमुखाकृति॥ १६ ॥

अथ वीरासनम्।

एकपादमथैकस्मिन्विन्यसेदूरुसंस्थितम्।
इतरस्मिंस्तथा पश्चाद्वीरासनमितीरितम्[4]॥ १७ ॥

---

१ कारणं. २ करौ. ३ धरं. ४ मिदं विदुः.

अथ धनुरासनम्।

प्रसार्य्य पादौ भुवि दण्डरूपौ करौ[1] च पृष्ठे[2] धृतपादयुग्मम्।
कृत्वा धनुस्[3]तुल्[4]यपरिवर्त्तिताङ्गं निगद्य योगी[5] धनुरासनं तत् १८

अथ मृतासनम्।

उत्तानं शववद्भूमौ शयानन्तु शवासनम्।
शवासनं श्रमहरं चित्तविश्रान्तिकारणम्॥ १९॥

अथ गुप्तासनम्।

जानूर्वोरन्तरे पादौ कृत्वा पादौ च गोपयेत्।
पादोपरि च संस्थाप्य गुदं गुप्तासनं विदुः॥ २०॥

अथ मत्स्यासनम्।

मुक्तपद्मासनं कृत्वा उत्तानशयनश्चरेत्।
कूर्परभ्यां शिरो वेष्टचं मत्स्यासनन्तु रोगहा॥ २१॥

अथ मत्स्येन्द्रासनम्।

उदरं पश्चिमाभासं कृत्वा तिष्ठति यत्नतः।
नम्राङ्गं वामपादं हि दक्षजानूपरि न्यसेत्॥ २२॥
तत्र याम्यं कूर्परञ्च याम्यकरे च वक्त्रकम्।
भ्रुवोर्मध्ये गता दृष्टिः पीठं मात्स्येन्द्रमुच्यते॥ २३॥

अथ गोरक्षासनम्।

जानूर्व्वोरन्तरे पादौ उत्तानौ व्यक्तसंस्थितौ।
गुल्फौ चाच्छाद्य हस्ताभ्यामुत्तानाभ्यां प्रयत्नतः॥ २४॥

---

१ कर्णौ. २ पृष्टवा. ३ तु. ४ ल्यं. ५ ते वै.

कण्ठसंकोचनं कृत्वा नासाग्रमवलोकयेत्।
गोरक्षासनमित्याह योगिनां सिद्धिकारणम्[1] ॥ २५ ॥

अथ पश्चिमोत्तानासनम्।

प्रसार्य पादौ भुवि दण्डरूपौ
संन्यस्तभालं चितियुग्ममध्ये।
यत्नेन पादौ च धृतौ कराभ्यां
योगीन्द्रपीठं पश्चिमोत्तानमाहुः ॥ २६ ॥

अथ उत्कटासनम्।

अङ्गुष्ठाभ्यामवष्टभ्य धरां गुल्फौ च खे गतौ।
तत्रोपरि गुदं न्यस्य विज्ञेयमुत्कटासनम् ॥ २७ ॥

अथ सङ्कटासनम्।

वामपादं चितेर्मूलं संन्यस्य धरणीतले।
पाददण्डेन याम्येन वेष्टयेद्वामपादकम्।
जानुयुग्मे करयुग्ममेतत्सङ्कटमासनम् ॥ २८ ॥

अथ मयूरासनम्।

धरामवष्टभ्य करतलाभ्यां[2]
तत्कूर्परे स्थापितनाभिपार्श्वम्।
उच्चासने दण्डवदुत्थितः खे
मायूरमेतत्प्रवदन्ति पीठम् ॥ २९ ॥
बहु कदशनभुक्तं भस्म कुर्यादशेषं
जनयति जठराग्निं जारयेत्कालकूटम्।

---

१ कम्. २ द्वयेन.

हरति सकलरोगानाशु गुल्मज्वरादी-
न्भवति विगतदोषमासनं श्रीमयूरम् ॥ ३० ॥

अथ कुक्कुटासनम् ।

पद्मासनं समासाद्य[1] जानूर्वोरन्तरे करौ ।
कूर्पराभ्यां समासीन उच्चस्थः कुक्कुटासनम् ॥ ३१ ॥

अथ कूर्मासनम् ।

गुल्फौ च वृषणस्याधो व्युत्क्रमेण समाहितौ[2] ।
ऋजुकायशिरोग्रीवं कूर्मासनमितीरितम् ॥ ३२ ॥

अथ उत्तानकूर्मकासनम् ।

कुक्कुटासनबन्धस्थं कराभ्यां धृतकन्धरम् ।
शेते कूर्मवदुत्तानमेतदुत्तानकूर्मकम् ॥ ३३ ॥

अथ मण्डूकासनम् ।

पादतलौ पृष्ठदेशे अङ्गुष्ठे[3] द्वे[3] च संस्पृशेत् ।
जानुयुग्मं पुरस्कृत्य साधयेन्मण्डूकासनम्[4] ॥ ३४ ॥(५)

अथ उत्तानमण्डूकासनम् ।

मण्डूकासनमध्यस्थं कूर्पराभ्यां धृतं शिरः ।
शेते भेकवदुत्तानमेतदुत्तानमण्डुकम् ॥ ३५ ॥

अथ वृक्षासनम् ।

वामोरुमूलदेशे च याम्यं पादं निधाय तु ।
तिष्ठेत्तु वृक्षवद्भूमौ वृक्षासनमिदं विदुः[6] ॥ ३६ ॥

---

१ ध्य. २ तः. ३ ष्ठाग्रे. ४ डु. (५) आसनभेदकथकश्लोके उत्तानमण्डुकासनस्य पूर्वं कथितत्वेपि तज्ज्ञाने मण्डूकासनप्रयोगज्ञानस्यापेक्षितत्वात् तत्पूर्वमेतत्पाठः. ६ तदेव हि.

अथ गरुडासनम्।

जङ्घोरुभ्यां धरां पीड्य स्थिरकायो द्विजानुना।
जानूपरि करद्वन्द्वं गरुडासनमुच्यते ॥ ३७ ॥

अथ वृषासनम्।

याम्यगुल्फे पायुमूलं वामभागे पदेतरम्।
विपरीतं स्पृशेद्भूमिं वृषासनमिदं [1]भवेत् ॥ ३८ ॥

अथ शलभासनम्।

अध्यास्यः शेते करयुग्मं वक्षे
भूमिमवष्टभ्य करयोस्तलाभ्याम्।
पादौ च शून्ये च वितस्ति चोर्ध्वं
वदन्ति पीठं शलभं मुनीन्द्राः ॥ ३९ ॥

अथ मकरासनम्।

अध्यास्यः शेते हृदयं निधाय
भूमौ च पादौ च प्रसार्यमाणौ।
शिरश्च धृत्वा करदण्डयुग्मे
देहाग्निकारं मकरासनं तत् ॥ ४० ॥

अथ उष्ट्रासनम्।

अध्यास्यः शेते पदयुग्मव्यस्तं
पृष्ठे निधायापि धृतं कराभ्याम्।
आकुञ्चयेच्चर्ममुदरस्य गाढ-
मौष्ट्रञ्च पीठं योगिनो वदन्ति ॥ ४१ ॥

---

१ युगिनो.

अथ भुजङ्गासनम् ।

पादादिनाभिपर्यन्तमधोभूमौ विनिन्यसेत्[१] ।
करतलाभ्यां धरां धृत्वा ऊर्ध्वशीर्षः फणीव हि ॥४२॥
देहाग्निर्वर्द्धते नित्यं सर्वरोग[२]विनाशनम्[३] ।
जागर्ति भुजगी देवी भुजगासनसाधनात् ॥ ४३ ॥

अथ योगासनम् ।

उत्तानौ चरणौ कृत्वा संस्थाप्य जानुनोपरि ।
आसनोपरि संस्थाप्य उत्तानं करयुग्मकम् ॥ ४४ ॥
पूरकैर्वायुमाकृष्य नासाग्रमवलोकयेत् ।
योगासनं भवेदेतद्योगिनां योगसाधने ॥ ४५ ॥

इति श्रीघेरण्डसंहितायां घटस्थयोगे घेरण्डचण्ड-संवादे आसनप्रयोगो नाम द्वितीयोपदेशः समाप्तः ।

तृतीयोपदेशः ।

अथ मुद्राकथनम् ।

घेरण्ड उवाच—

महामुद्रा नभोमुद्रा उड्डीयानं ज[४]लन्धरम् ।
मूलबन्धं महाबन्धं महावेधश्च खेचरी ॥ १ ॥
विपरीतकरी योनिर्वज्रोली शक्तिचालनी ।
ताडागी माण्डुकी मुद्रा शाम्भवी पञ्चधारणा ॥ २ ॥

---

१ च. २ ग. ३ येत्. ४ जा. ५ भा च. ६ त.

अश्विनी पाशिनी काकी मातङ्गी च भुजङ्गिनी ।
पञ्चविंशति[1] मुद्राणि[2] सिद्धिदानीहे योगिनाम् ॥ ३ ॥

अथ मुद्राणां फलकथनम् ।

मुद्राणां पटलं देवि कथितं तव सन्निधौ ।
येन विज्ञातमात्रेण सर्वसिद्धिः प्रजायते ॥ ४ ॥
गोपनीयं प्रयत्नेन न देयं यस्य कस्यचित् ।
प्रीतिदं योगिनाञ्चैव दुर्लभं मरुतामपि ॥ ५ ॥

अथ महामुद्राकथनम् ।

पायुमूलं वामगुल्फे संपीड्य दृढयत्नतः ।
याम्यपादं प्रसार्याथ करे धृतपदाङ्गुलः ॥ ६ ॥
कण्ठसंकोचनं कृत्वा भ्रुवोर्मध्यं[3] निरीक्षयेत् ।
पूरकैर्वायुं संपूर्य महामुद्रा निगद्यते ॥ ७ ॥

अथ महामुद्राफलकथनम् ।

क्षयकासं गुदावर्त्तं प्लीहाजीर्णं ज्वरं तथा ।
नाशयेत्सर्वरोगांश्च महामुद्रा च साधनात् ॥ ८ ॥

अथ नभोमुद्राकथनम् ।

यत्र यत्र स्थितो योगी सर्वकार्येषु[4] सर्वदा ।
ऊर्ध्वजिह्वः स्थिरो भूत्वा धारयेत् पवनं सदा ।
नभोमुद्रा भवेदेषा योगिनां रोगनाशिनी ॥ ९ ॥

अथ उड्डीयानबन्धः ।

उदरे पश्चिमं तानं नाभेरूर्ध्वं तु कारयेत् ।

---

१ श्च. २ ति. ३ ध्ये. ४ कर्मसु.

उड्डानं कुरुते यस्मादविश्रान्तं महाखगः।
उड्डीयानं त्वसौ बन्धो मृत्युमातङ्गकेसरी ॥ १० ॥

अथ उड्डीयानबन्धस्य फलकथनम्।

समग्राद्बन्धनाद् ह्येतदुड्डीयानं विशिष्यते।
उड्डीयाने समभ्यस्ते मुक्तिः स्वाभाविकी भवेत् ॥ ११ ॥

अथ जालन्धरबन्धकथनम्।

कण्ठसंकोचनं कृत्वा चिबुकं हृदये न्यसेत्।
जालन्धरे कृते बन्धे षोडशाधारबन्धनम्।
जालन्धरमहामुद्रा मृत्योश्च क्षयकारिणी ॥ १२ ॥

अथ जालन्धरबन्धस्य फलकथनम्।

सिद्धं जालन्धरं बन्धं योगिनां सिद्धिदायकम्।
षण्मासमभ्यसेद्यो हि स सिद्धो नात्र संशयः ॥ १३ ॥

अथ मूलबन्धकथनम्।

पार्ष्णिना वामपादस्य योनिमाकुञ्चयेत्ततः।
नाभिग्रन्थिं मेरुदण्डे संपीड्य यत्नतः सुधीः ॥ १४ ॥
मेढ्रं दक्षिणगुल्फे तु दृढबन्धं समाचरेत्।
जराविनाशिनी मुद्रा मूलबन्धो निगद्यते ॥ १५ ॥

अथ मूलबन्धस्य फलकथनम्।

संसारसमुद्रं तर्त्तुमभिलषति यः पुमान्।
विरले सुगुप्तो भूत्वा मुद्रामेतां समभ्यसेत् ॥ १६ ॥
अभ्यासाद् बन्धनस्यास्य मरुत्सिद्धिर्भवेद् ध्रुवम्।
साधयेद् यत्नतो तर्हि मौनी तु विजितालसः ॥ १७ ॥

---

१ अमृता.

अथ महाबन्धकथनम्।

वामपादस्य गुल्फेन पायुमूलं निरोधयेत्।
दक्षपादेन तद्गुल्फं संपीड्य यत्नतः सुधीः॥ १८॥
शनैः शनैश्चालयेत् पार्ष्णिं योनिमाकुञ्चयेच्छनैः।
जालन्धरे[1] धारयेत् प्राणं महाबन्धो[2] निगद्यते॥ १९॥

अथ महाबन्धस्य फलकथनम्।

महाबन्धः परो बन्धो जरामरणनाशनः।
प्रसादादस्य बन्धस्य साधयेत् सर्ववाञ्छितम्॥ २०॥

अथ महावेधकथनम्।

रूपयौवनलावण्यं नारीणां पुरुषं विना।
मूलबन्धमहाबन्धौ महावेधं विना तथा॥ २१॥
महाबन्धं समासाद्य उड्डानकुम्भकं चरेत्।
महावेधः समाख्यातो योगिनां सिद्धिदायकः॥ २२॥

अथ महावेधस्य फलकथनम्।

महाबन्धमूलबन्धौ महावेधसमन्वितौ।
प्रत्यहं कुरुते यस्तु स योगी योगवित्तमः॥ २३॥
न मृत्युतो भयं तस्य न जरा तस्य विद्यते।
गोपनीयः प्रयत्नेन वेधोयं योगिपुङ्गवैः॥ २४॥

अथ खेचरीमुद्राकथनम्।

जिह्वाधो नाडीं संछिन्नां रसनां चालयेत् सदा।
दोहयेन्नवनीतेन लौहयन्त्रेण कर्षयेत्॥ २५॥

---

१ रं. २ धं. ३ पूरकं.

एवं नित्यं सम[1]भ्यासाल्लम्बिका दीर्घतां व्रजेत् ।
यावद्गच्छेद् भ्रुवोर्मध्ये तदागच्छति[2] खेचरी ॥ २६ ॥
रसनां तालुम[3]ध्ये तु शनैः शनैः प्रवे[4]शयेत् ।
कपालकुहरे जिह्वा प्रविष्टा विपरीतगा ।
भ्रुवोर्मध्ये गता दृष्टिर्मुद्रा भवति खेचरी ॥ २७ ॥

अथ खेचरीमुद्रायाः फलकथनम् ।

न च मूर्च्छा क्षुधा तृष्णा नैवालस्यं प्रजायते ।
न च रोगो जरा मृत्युर्देवदेहः स जायते ॥ २८ ॥
नाग्निना दह्यते गात्रं न शोषयति मारुतः ।
न देहं क्लेदयन्त्यापो दंशयेन्न भुजङ्गमः ॥ २९ ॥
लावण्यञ्च भवेद्गात्रे समाधिर्जायते ध्रुवम् ।
कपालवक्त्रसंयोगे रसना रसमाप्नुयात् ॥ ३० ॥
नानारससमुद्भूतमानन्दं च दिने दिने ।
आदौ लवणक्षारञ्च ततस्तिक्तकषायकम् ॥ ३१ ॥
नवनीतं घृतं क्षीरं दधि तक्रमधूनि च ।
द्राक्षारसञ्च पीयूषं जायते रसनोदकम् ॥ ३२ ॥

अथ विपरीतकरणीमुद्राकथनम् ।

नाभिमूले वसेत् सूर्यस्तालुमूले च चन्द्रमाः ।
अमृतं ग्रसते सूर्यस्ततो मृत्युवशो नरः ॥ ३३ ॥
ऊर्ध्वं च योजयत् सूर्यञ्चन्द्रञ्च अध आनयेत् ।
विपरीतकरी मुद्रा सर्वतन्त्रेषु गोपिता ॥ ३४ ॥

---

१ मा. २ सिध्यति. ३ रंध्रे. ४ प्रसारयेत्.

भूमौ शिरश्च संस्थाप्य करयुग्मं समाहितः।
ऊर्ध्वपादः स्थिरो भूत्वा विपरीतकरी मता॥ ३५॥

अथ विपरीतकरणीमुद्रायाः फलकथनम्।

मुद्रां च साधयेन्नित्यं जरां मृत्युश्च नाशयेत्।
स सिद्धः सर्वलोकेषु प्रलयेऽपि न सीदति॥ ३६॥

अथ योनिमुद्राकथनम्।

सिद्धासनं समासाद्य कर्णचक्षुर्नासामुखम्।
अङ्गुष्ठतर्जनीमध्यानामादिभिश्च साधयेत्॥ ३७॥
काकोभिः[1] प्राणं संकृष्य अपाने योजयेत्ततः।
षट्चक्राणि क्रमाद्ध्यात्वा हुं[2] हंस[3]मनुना सुधीः॥ ३८
चैतन्यमानयेद्देवीं निद्रिता या भुजङ्गिनी।
जीवेन सहितां शक्तिं समुत्थाप्य कराम्बुजे॥ ३९॥
शक्तिमयः स्वयं भूत्वा परं शिवेन सङ्गमम्।
नानासुखं विहारञ्च चिन्तयेत् परमं सुखम्॥ ४०॥
शिवशक्तिसमायोगादेकान्तं भुवि भावयेत्।
आनन्दमानसो भूत्वा अहं ब्रह्मेति संभवेत्॥ ४१॥
योनिमुद्रा परा गोप्या देवानामपि दुर्लभा।
सकृत्तु लब्धसंसिद्धिः समाधिस्थः स एव हि॥ ४२॥

अथ योनिमुद्राफलकथनम्।

ब्रह्महा भ्रूणहा चैव सुरापी गुरुतल्पगः।
एतैः पापैर्न लिप्येत योनिमुद्रानिबन्धनात्॥ ४३॥

---

१ काकिना–काकीवत्. २ हूं. ३सो. ४ स्म.–स्मा. ५ स्वं–नं. ६भाव.

यानि पापानि घोराणि उपपापानि यानि च।
तानि सर्वाणि नश्यन्ति योनिमुद्रानिबन्धनात्।
तस्मादभ्यसनं कुर्याद्यदि मुक्तिं समिच्छति ॥ ४४ ॥

अथ वज्रोलीमुद्राकथनम्।

धरामवष्टभ्य करयोस्तले[1]भ्यामूर्ध्वं क्षिपेत्पादयुगं शिरः खे।
शक्तिप्रबोधाय चिरजीवनाय वज्रोलिमुद्रां मुनयो वदन्ति ४५

अथ वज्रोलीमुद्रायाः फलकथनम्।

अयं योगो योगश्रेष्ठो योगिनां मुक्तिकारणम्।
अयं हितप्रदो योगो योगिनां सिद्धिदायकः ॥ ४६ ॥
एतद्योगप्रसादेन बिन्दुसिद्धिर्भवेद् ध्रुवम्।
सिद्धे बिन्दौ महायत्ने किं न सिद्ध्यति भूतले ॥ ४७ ॥
भोगेन महता युक्तो यदि मुद्रां समाचरेत्।
तथापि सकला सिद्धिस्तस्य भवति निश्चितम् ॥ ४८ ॥

अथ शक्तिचालनीमुद्राकथनम्।

मूलाधारे आत्मशक्तिः कुण्डली परदेवता।
शयिता[2] भुजगाकारा सार्द्ध[3]त्रिवलयान्विता ॥ ४९ ॥
यावत् सा निद्रिता देहे तावज्जीवः पशुर्यथा।
ज्ञानं न जायते तावत् कोटियोगं समभ्यसेत् ॥ ५० ॥
उद्घाटयेत् कवाटं[4] च यथा कुञ्चिकया हठात्।
कुण्डलिन्याः प्रबोधेन ब्रह्मद्वारं प्रभेदयेत्[5] ॥ ५१ ॥
नाभिं[6] संवेष्ट्य वस्त्रेण न च नग्नो बहिस्थितः।
गोपनीयगृहे स्थित्वा शक्तिचालनमभ्यसेत् ॥ ५२ ॥

---

१ करद्वयेन. २ संयुता. ३ ऊर्ध्व. ४ कपाटं. ५ वि. ६ नातिबृहद्वेष्टनं च.

वितस्तिप्रमितं दीर्घं विस्तारे चतुरङ्गुलम्।
मृदुलं धवलं सूक्ष्मं वेष्टनाम्बरलक्षणम्।
एवमम्बरयुक्तश्च कटिसूत्रेण योजयेत्॥ ५३॥
भस्मना गात्रं संलिप्य सिद्धासनं समाचरेत्।
नासाभ्यां प्राणमाकृष्य अपाने योजवेद् बलात्॥ ५४॥
तावदाकुञ्चयेद्गुह्यं शनैरश्विनीमुद्रया।
यावद्गच्छेत् सुषुम्नायां वायुः प्रकाशयेद्धठात्॥ ५५॥
तदा वायुप्रबन्धेन कुम्भिका च भुजङ्गिनी।
बद्धश्वासस्ततो भूत्वा ऊर्ध्वमार्गं प्रपद्यते॥ ५६॥
विना शक्तिचालनेन योनिमुद्रा न सिद्ध्यति।
आदौ चालनमभ्यस्य योनिमुद्रां समभ्यसेत्॥ ५७॥
इति ते कथितं चण्डकपाले शक्तिचालनम्।
गोपनीयं प्रयत्नेन दिने दिने समभ्यसेत्॥ ५८॥

अथ शक्तिचालनीमुद्रायाः फलकथनम्।

मुद्रेयं परमा गोप्या जरामरणनाशिनी।
तस्मादभ्यसनं कार्यं योगिभिः सिद्धिकाङ्क्षिभिः॥५९॥
नित्यं योऽभ्यसते योगी सिद्धिस्तस्य करे स्थिता।
तस्य विग्रहसिद्धिः स्याद्रोगाणां संक्षयो भवेत्॥ ६०॥

अथ तडागीमुद्राकथनम्।

उदरं पश्चिमोत्तानं कृत्वा च तडागाकृति।
ताडागी सा परा मुद्रा जरामृत्युविनाशिनी॥ ६१॥

---

१ सा, २ प्रकारं—प्रकाशं.

अथ माण्डुकीमुद्राकथनम् ।

मुखं समुद्रितं कृत्वा जिह्वामूलं प्रचालयेत् ।
शनैर्ग्रसेदमृतं तन्माण्डुकीं मुद्रिकां विदुः ॥ ६२ ॥

अथ माण्डुकीमुद्रायाः फलकथनम् ।

वलितं पलितं नैव जायते नित्ययौवनम् ।
न केशे जायते पाको यः कुर्यान्नित्यमाण्डुकीम् ॥ ६३ ॥

अथ शाम्भवीमुद्राकथनम् ।

नेत्राञ्जनं समालोक्य आत्मारामं निरीक्षयेत् ।
सा भवेच्छाम्भवी मुद्रा सर्वतन्त्रेषु गोपिता ॥ ६४ ॥

अथ शाम्भवीमुद्रायाः फलकथनम् ।

वेदशास्त्रपुराणानि सामान्यगणिका इव ।
इयं तु शाम्भवी मुद्रा गुप्ता कुलवधूरिव ॥ ६५ ॥
स एव आदिनाथश्च स च नारायणः स्वयम् ।
स च ब्रह्मा सृष्टिकारी यो मुद्रां वेत्ति शाम्भवीम् ॥ ६६ ॥
सत्यं सत्यं पुनः सत्यं सत्यमुक्तं महेश्वर ।
शाम्भवीं यो विजानीयात् स च ब्रह्म न चान्यथा ॥ ६७ ॥

अथ पञ्चधारणामुद्राकथनम् ।

कथिता शाम्भवी मुद्रा शृणुष्व पञ्चधारणाम् ।
धारणानि[1] समासाद्य[2] किं न सिध्यति भूतले ॥ ६८ ॥
अनेन नरदेहेन स्वर्गेषु गमनागमम् ।
मनोगतिर्भवेत्तस्य खेचरत्वं न चान्यथा ॥ ६९ ॥

---

१ धारणां च. २ ध्य.

अथ पार्थिवीधारणामुद्राकथनम्।

यत्तत्त्वं हरितालदेशरचितं भौमं[1] लकारान्वितं

वेदास्त्रं[2] कमलासनेन सहितं कृत्वा हृदि स्थायिनम्[3]।

प्राणं तत्र विलीय पञ्च घटिकाश्चित्तान्वितं धारये-

देषा स्तम्भकरी सदा क्षितिजयं कुर्यादधोधारणा ७०

अथ पार्थिवीधारणामुद्रायाः फलकथनम्।

पार्थिवीधारणामुद्रां यः करोति च नित्यशः।

मृत्युञ्जयः स्वयं सोपि स सिद्धो विचरेद् भुवि ॥ ७१ ॥

अथ आम्भसीधारणामुद्राकथनम्।

शङ्खेन्दुप्रतिमञ्च कुन्दधवलं तत्त्वं किलालं शुभं

तत्पीयुषवकारबीजसहितं युक्तं सदा विष्णुना।

प्राणं तत्र विलीय पञ्चघटिकाश्चित्तान्वितं धारयेदेषा

दुःसहतापपापहरणी स्यादाम्भसी धारणा ॥७२॥

अथ आम्भसीमुद्रायाः फलकथनम्।

आम्भसीं परमां मुद्रां यो जानाति स योगवित्।

जले च गभीरे घोरे मरणं तस्य नो भवेत् ॥ ७३ ॥

इयं तु परमा मुद्रा गोपनीया प्रयत्नतः।

प्रकाशात् सिद्धिहानिः स्यात् सत्यं वच्मि च तत्त्वतः ७४

अथ आग्नेयीधारणामुद्राकथनम्।

यन्नाभिस्थितमिन्द्रगोपसदृशं बीजं त्रिकोणान्वितं

तत्त्वं तेजोमयं प्रदीप्तमरुणं रुद्रेण यत् सिद्धिदम्।

---

१ हेमा. २ थं. ३ स्थापितम्.

प्राणं तत्र विलीय पञ्चघटिकाश्चित्तान्वितं धारये-
देषा कालगभीरभीतिहरणी वैश्वानरी धारणा ७५

अथ आग्नेयीधारणामुद्रायाः फलकथनम् ।

प्रदीप्ते ज्वलिते वह्नौ यदि पतति साधकः ।
एतन्मुद्राप्रसादेन स जीवति न मृत्युभाक् ॥ ७६ ॥

अथ वायवीधारणामुद्राकथनम् ।

यद्भिन्नाञ्जनपु[1]ञ्जसन्निभमिदं धूम्रावभा[2]सं प[2]रं
तत्त्वं स[3]त्त्वमयं यकारसहितं यत्रेश्वरो देवता ।
प्राणं तत्र विलीय पञ्चघटिकाश्चित्तान्वितं धारये-
देषा खे गमनं करोति यमिनां स्याद्वायवी धारणा ७७

अथ वायवीधारणामुद्रायाः फलकथनम् ।

इयं तु परमा मुद्रा जरामृत्युविनाशिनी ।
वायुना म्रियते नापि खे गतेश्च प्रदायिनी ॥ ७८ ॥
शठाय भक्तिहीनाय न देया यस्य कस्यचित् ।
दत्ते च सिद्धिहानिः स्यात् सत्यं वच्मि च चण्ड ते ॥७९॥

अथ आकाशीधारणामुद्राकथनम् ।

यत् सिन्धौ[4] वरशुद्धवारिसदृशं व्योमं[5] परं भासितं
तत्त्वं देवसदाशिवेन सहितं बीजं हकारान्वितम् ।
प्राणं तत्र विलीय पञ्चघटिकाश्चित्तान्वितं धारये-
देषा मोक्षकवाटभेदनकरी कुर्यान्नभोधारणाम् ॥ ८० ॥

---

१ पुष्प. २ वृत्तं भ्रुवोरन्तरे. ३ सत्य. ४ धोः. ५ प्रतिशुद्ध.
६ व्योम्नः.

अथ आकाशीधारणामुद्रायाः फलकथनम्।

आकाशीधारणां मुद्रां यो वेत्ति सच योगवित्।
न मृत्युर्जायते तस्य प्रलये नावसीदति ॥ ८१ ॥

अथ अश्विनीमुद्राकथनम्।

आकुञ्चयेद् गुदद्वारं प्रकाशयेत् पुनः पुनः।
सा भवेदश्विनी मुद्रा शक्तिप्रबोधकारिणी ॥ ८२ ॥

अश्विनीमुद्रायाः फलकथनम्।

अश्विनी परमा मुद्रा गुह्यरोगविनाशिनी।
बलपुष्टिकरी चैव अकालमरणं हरेत् ॥ ८३ ॥

अथ पाशिनीमुद्राकथनम्।

कण्ठ[1]पृष्ठे क्षिपेत् पादौ पाशवद् दृढबन्धनम्।
सा एव पाशिनी मुद्रा शक्तिप्रबोधकारिणी ॥ ८४ ॥

अथ पाशिनीमुद्रायाः फलकथनम्।

पाशिनी महती मुद्रा बलपुष्टिविधायिनी।
साधनीया प्रयत्नेन साधकैः सिद्धिकाङ्क्षिभिः ॥ ८५ ॥

अथ काकीमुद्राकथनम्।

काकचञ्चु[2]वदास्येन पिबेद्वायुं शनैः शनैः।
काकीमुद्रा भवेदेषा सर्वरोगविनाशिनी ॥ ८६ ॥

अथ काकीमुद्रायाः फलकथनम्।

काकीमुद्रा परा मुद्रा सर्वतन्त्रेषु गोपिता।
अस्याः प्रसादमात्रेण न रोगी काकवद् भवेत् ॥ ८७ ॥

---

१ स्कंध. २ चू.

अथ मातङ्गिनीमुद्राकथनम् ।

कण्ठमग्ने[1] जले स्थित्वा नासाभ्यां जलमाहरेत् ।
मुखान्निर्गमयेत् पश्चात् पुनर्वक्त्रेण चाहरेत् ॥ ८८ ॥
नासाभ्यां रेचयेत् पश्चात् कुर्यादेवं पुनः पुनः ।
मातङ्गिनी परा मुद्रा जरामृत्युविनाशिनी ॥ ८९ ॥

अथ मातङ्गिनीमुद्रायाः फलकथनम् ।

विरले निर्जने देशे स्थित्वा चैकाग्रमानसः ।
कुर्यान्मातङ्गिनीं मुद्रां मातङ्ग इव जायते ॥ ९० ॥
यत्र यत्र स्थितो रोगी सुखमत्यन्तमश्नुते ।
तस्मात् सर्वप्रयत्नेन साधयेन्मुद्रिकां पराम् ॥ ९१ ॥

अथ भुजङ्गिनीमुद्राकथनम् ।

वक्त्रं किञ्चित् सुप्रसार्य चानिलं गलया पिबेत् ।
सा भवेद् भुजगी मुद्रा जरामृत्युविनाशिनी ॥ ९२ ॥

अथ भुजङ्गिनीमुद्रायाः फलकथनम् ।

यावन्त उदरे रोगा अजीर्णादि विशेषतः ।
तत् सर्वं नाशयेदाशु यत्र मुद्रा भुजङ्गिनी ॥ ९३ ॥

अथ मुद्राणां फलकथनम् ।

इदं तु मुद्रापटलं कथितं चण्ड ते शुभम् ।
वल्लभं सर्वसिद्धानां जरामरणनाशनम् ॥ ९४ ॥
शठाय भक्तिहीनाय न देयं यस्य कस्यचित् ।
गोपनीयं प्रयत्नेन दुर्लभं मरुतामपि ॥ ९५ ॥

---

1 म.

ऋजवे शान्तचित्ताय गुरुभक्तिपराय च।
कुलीनाय प्रदातव्यं भोगमुक्तिप्रदायकम् ॥ ९६ ॥
मुद्राणां पटलं ह्येतत् सर्वव्याधिविनाशनम्।
नित्यमभ्यासशीलस्य जठराग्निविवर्धनम् ॥ ९७ ॥
न तस्य जायते मृत्युर्नास्य जरादिकं तथा।
नाग्निजलभयं तस्य वायोरपि कुतो भयम् ॥ ९८ ॥
कासः श्वासः प्लीहा कुष्ठं श्लेष्मरोगाश्च विंशतिः।
मुद्राणां साधनाच्चैव विनश्यन्ति न संशयः ॥ ९९ ॥
वहुना किमिहोक्तेन सारं वच्मि च चण्ड ते।
नास्ति मुद्रासमं किञ्चित् सिद्धिदं क्षितिमण्डले ॥१००॥

इति श्रीघेरण्डसंहितायां घेरण्डचण्डसंवादे घटस्थ-
योगप्रकरणे मुद्राप्रयोगो नाम तृतीयोपदेशः।

चतुर्थोपदेशः।

घेरण्ड उवाच—

अथातः संप्रवक्ष्यामि प्रत्याहारकमुत्तमम्।
यस्य विज्ञानमात्रेण कामादिरिपुनाशनम् ॥ १ ॥
यतो यतो निश्चरति मनश्चञ्चलमस्थिरम्।
ततस्ततो नियम्यैतदात्मन्येव वशं नयेत् ॥ २ ॥
यत्र यत्र गता दृष्टिर्मनस्तत्र प्रगच्छति।
ततः प्रत्याहरेदेतदात्मन्येव वशं नयेत् ॥ ३ ॥

पुरस्कारं तिरस्कारं सुश्राव्यं वा भयानकम् ।
मनस्तस्मान्नियम्यैतदात्मन्येव वशं नयेत् ॥ ४ ॥
शीतं वापि तथा चोष्णं यन्मनस्पर्शयोगतः ।
तस्मात्प्रत्याहरेदेतदात्मन्येव वशं नयेत् ॥ ५ ॥
सुगन्धे वापि दुर्गन्धे घ्राणेषु जायते मनः ।
तस्मात् प्रत्याहरेदेतदात्मन्येव वशं नयेत् ॥ ६ ॥
मधुराम्लकतिक्तादिरसं गतं यदा मनः ।
तस्मात् प्रत्याहरेदेतदात्मन्येव वशं नयेत् ॥ ७ ॥

इति श्रीघेरण्डसंहितायां घेरण्डचण्डसंवादे घटस्थ-
योगे प्रत्याहारप्रयोगो नाम चतुर्थोपदेशः ।

पञ्चमोपदेशः ।

घेरण्ड उवाच—

अथातः संप्रवक्ष्यामि प्राणायामस्य यद्विधिम् ।
यस्य साधनमात्रेण देवतुल्यो भवेन्नरः ॥ १ ॥
आदौ स्थानं तथा कालं मिताहारं तथापरम् ।
नाडीशुद्धिं ततः पश्चात् प्राणायामं च साधयेत् ॥ २ ॥

अथ स्थाननिर्णयः ।

दूरदेशे तथारण्ये राजधान्यां जनान्तिके ।
योगारम्भं न कुर्वीत कृतश्चेत् सिद्धिहा भवेत् ॥ ३ ॥

अविश्वासं दूरदेशे अरण्ये रक्षिवर्जितम्।
लोकारण्ये प्रकाशश्च तस्मात् त्रीणि विवर्जयेत् ॥ ४ ॥
सुदेशे धार्मिके राज्ये सुभिक्षे निरुपद्रवे।
तत्रैकं कुटीरं कृत्वा प्राचीरैः परिवेष्टितम् ॥ ५ ॥
वापीकूपतडागं च प्राचीरमध्यवर्ति च।
नात्युच्चं नातिनिम्नं च कुटीरं कीटवर्जितम् ॥ ६ ॥
सम्यग्गोमयलिप्तं च कुर्याद्रन्ध्रविवर्जितम्।
एवं स्थानेषु गुप्तेषु प्राणायामं समभ्यसेत्[२] ॥ ७ ॥

अथ कालनिर्णयः।

हेमन्ते शिशिरे ग्रीष्मे वर्षायां च ऋतौ[३] तथा[३]।
योगारम्भं न कुर्वीत कृते योगो हि रोगदः ॥ ८ ॥
वसन्ते शरदि प्रोक्तं योगारम्भं समाचरेत्।
तथा योगो भवेत् सिद्धो रोगान्मुक्तो भवेद् ध्रुवम् ॥९॥
चैत्रादिफाल्गुनान्ते च माघादिफाल्गुनान्तिके।
द्वौ द्वौ मासौ ऋतुभागौ अनुभावश्चतुश्चतुः ॥ १० ॥
वसन्तश्चैत्रवैशाखौ ज्येष्ठाषाढौ च ग्रीष्मकौ।
वर्षा श्रावणभाद्राभ्यां शरदाश्विनकार्तिकौ।
मार्गपौषौ च हेमन्तः शिशिरो माघफाल्गुनौ ॥ ११ ॥
अनुभावं प्रवक्ष्यामि ऋतूनां च यथोदितम्।
माघादिमाधवान्तेषु वसन्तानुभवं विदुः ॥ १२ ॥

---

१ भक्ष्य. २ समाचरेत्. ३ चतुर्षु च. ४ श्चैव. ५ तदा.

चैत्रादि चाषाढान्तं च निदाघानुभवं[1] विदुः ।
आषाढादि चाश्विनान्तं प्रावृषानुभवं विदुः ॥ १३ ॥
भाद्रादिमार्गशीर्षान्तं शरदोऽनुभवं विदुः ।
कार्तिकादिमाघमासान्तं हेमन्तानुभवं विदुः ।
मार्गादिचतुरो मासान् शिशिरानुभवं विदुः ॥ १४ ॥
वसन्ते वापि शरदि योगारम्भं समाचरेत् ।
तदा योगो भवेत् सिद्धो विनायासेन कथ्यते ॥ १५ ॥

अथ मिताहारः ।

मिताहारं विना यस्तु योगारम्भं तु कारयेत् ।
नानारोगो भवेत्तस्य किञ्चिद्योगो न सिध्यति ॥ १६ ॥
शाल्यन्नं यवपिष्टं वा गोधूमपिष्टकं तथा ।
मुद्गं माषचणकादि शुभ्रं च तूषवर्जितम् ॥ १७ ॥
पटोलं पनसं[2] मानं कक्कोलं[3] च शुकाशकम् ।
द्राढिकां[4] कर्कटीं रम्भां डुम्बरीं कण्टकण्टकम्[5] ॥ १८ ॥
आमरम्भां भालरम्भां रम्भादण्डं च मूलकम् ।
वार्ताकीं मूलकं ऋद्धिं[6] योगी भक्षणमाचरेत् ॥ १९ ॥
बालशाकं कालवाकं तथा पटोलपत्रकम् ।
पञ्चशाकं प्रशंसीयाद्वास्तूकं हिलमोचिकाम् ॥ २० ॥
शुद्धं सुमधुरं स्निग्धं उदरार्धविवर्जितम् ।
भुज्यते सुरसं प्रीत्या मिताहारमिमं विदुः ॥ २१ ॥

---

१ ग्रीष्मका. २ शूरणं. ३ कंकोलं. ४ टि. ५ कर्चुकम्. ६ सिंगीं —डिंगीं.

अन्नेन पूरयेदर्धं तोयेन तु तृतीयकम् ।
उदरस्य तुरीयांशं संरक्षेद्वायुचारणे ॥ २२ ॥
कट्वम्लं लवणं तिक्तं भृष्टं च दधि तक्रकम् ।
शाकोत्कटं तथा मद्यं तालं च पनसं तथा ॥ २३ ॥
कुलत्थं मसूरं पाण्डुं कूष्माण्डं शाकदण्डकम् ।
तुम्बीकोलकपित्थं च कण्टबिल्वं पलाशकम् ॥ २४ ॥
कदम्बं जम्बीरं बिम्बं लकुचं लशुनं विषम् ।
कामरङ्गं पियालं च हिङ्गुशाल्मलीकेमुकम् ॥ २५ ॥
योगारम्भे वर्जयेच्च पथस्त्रीवह्निसेवनम् ।
नवनीतं घृतं क्षीरं गुडं शर्करादि चैक्षवम् ॥ २६ ॥
पक्वरम्भां नारिकेलं दाडिम्बमशिवासवम् ।
द्राक्षाङ्कुलवनीं धात्रीं रसमाम्लविवर्जितम् ॥ २७ ॥
एलाजातिलवङ्गं च पौरुषं जम्बु जाम्बलम् ।
हरीतकीं खर्जूरं च योगी भक्षणमाचरेत् ॥ २८ ॥
लघुपाकं प्रियं स्निग्धं तथा धातुप्रपोषणम् ।
मनोऽभिलषितं योग्यं योगी भोजनमाचरेत् ॥ २९ ॥
काठिन्यं दुरितं पूतिमुष्णं पर्युषितं तथा ।
अतिशीतं चाति चोष्णं भक्ष्यं योगी विवर्जयेत् ॥ ३० ॥
प्रातःस्नानोपवासादि कायक्लेशविधिं तथा ।
एकाहारं निराहारं यामान्ते च न कारयेत् ॥ ३१ ॥
एवं विधिविधानेन प्राणायामं समाचरेत् ।

आरम्भे प्रथमे कुर्यात् क्षीराज्यं नित्यभोजनम् ।
मध्याह्ने चैव सायाह्ने भोजनद्वयमाचरेत् ॥ ३२ ॥

इति मिताहारः ।

अथ नाडीशुद्धिः ।

कुशासने मृगाजिने व्याघ्राजिने च कम्बले ।
स्थलासने[1] समासीनः प्राङ्मुखो वाप्युदङ्मुखः ।
नाडीशुद्धिं समासाद्य[2] प्राणायामं समभ्यसेत् ॥ ३३ ॥

चण्डकापालिरुवाच ।

नाडीशुद्धिं कथं कुर्यान्नाडीशुद्धिस्तु कीदृशी ।
तत् सर्वं श्रोतुमिच्छामि तद्वदस्व दयानिधे ॥ ३४ ॥

घेरण्ड उवाच—

मलाकुलासु नाडीषु मारुतो नैव गच्छति ।
प्राणायामः कथं सिध्येत्तत्त्वज्ञानं कथं भवेत्[3] ॥ ३५ ॥
तस्मादादौ नाडीशुद्धिं प्राणायामं ततोऽभ्यसेत् ।
नाडीशुद्धिर्द्विधा प्रोक्ता समनुर्निर्मनुस्तथा ॥ ३६ ॥
बीजेन समनुं कुर्यान्निर्मनुं धौतकर्मणा ।
धौतकर्म पुरा प्रोक्तं षट्कर्मसाधने यथा ॥ ३७ ॥
शृणुष्व समनुं चण्ड नाडीशुद्धिर्यथा भवेत् ।
उपविश्यासने योगी पद्मासनं समाचरेत् ॥ ३८ ॥
गुर्वादिन्यासनं कुर्याद् यथैव गुरुभाषितम् ।
नाडीशुद्धिं प्रकुर्वीत प्राणायामविशुद्धये[4] ॥ ३९ ॥

१ स्थूला. २ ध्य. ३ लभेत्. ४ पान.

वायुबीजं ततो ध्यात्वा धूम्रवर्णं सतेजसम् ।
चन्द्रेण[1] पूरयेद्वायुं बीजं षोडशकैः सुधीः[2] ॥ ४० ॥
चतुःषष्ट्या मात्रया च कुम्भकेनैव धारयेत् ।
द्वात्रिंशन्मात्रया वायुं सूर्यनाड्या च रेचयेत् ॥ ४१ ॥
नाभिमूलाद्वह्निमुत्थाप्य ध्यायेत्तेजोऽवनीयुतम् ।
वह्निबीजषोडशेन सूर्यनाड्या च पूरयेत् ॥ ४२ ॥
चतुःषष्ट्या मात्रया च कुम्भकेनैव धारयेत् ।
द्वात्रिंशन्मात्रया वायुं शशिनाड्या च रेचयेत् ॥४३॥
नासाग्रे शशधृग्बिम्बं ध्यात्वा ज्योत्स्नासमन्वितम् ।
ठं बीजषोडशेनैव इडया पूरयेन्मरुत् ॥ ४४ ॥
चतुःषष्ट्या मात्रया च वं बीजेनैव धारयेत् ।
अमृतं प्लावितं ध्यात्वा नाडीधौतं विभावयेत् ।
लकारेण द्वात्रिंशेन दृढं भाव्यं विरेचयेत् ॥ ४५ ॥
एवंविधां नाडीशुद्धिं कृत्वा नाडीं विशोधयेत् ।
दृढो[3] भूत्वासनं कृत्वा प्राणायामं समाचरेत् ॥ ४६ ॥
सहितः सूर्यभेदश्च उज्जायी शीतली तथा ।
भस्त्रिका भ्रामरी मूर्छा केवली चाष्टकुम्भिकाः ॥ ४७ ॥
सहितो द्विविधः प्रोक्तः सगर्भश्च निगर्भकः ।
सगर्भो बीजमुच्चार्य निगर्भो बीजवर्जितः ॥ ४८ ॥
प्राणायामं सगर्भं च प्रथमं कथयामि ते ।
सुखासने चोपविश्य प्राङ्मुखो वाप्युदङ्मुखः ॥ ४९ ॥

---

१ पूरयेद्वायुबीजेन चन्द्रेण षोडशैः. २ सुधीः. ३ दृढासनं ततः कृत्वा.

ध्यायेद्विधिं रजोगुणं रक्तवर्णमवर्णकम् ।
इडया पूरयेद्वायुं मात्रया षोडशैः सुधीः ॥ ५० ॥
पूरकान्ते कुम्भकाद्ये कर्त्तव्यस्तूड्डीयानकः ।
सत्त्वमयं हरिं ध्यात्वा उकारं कृष्णवर्णकम् ॥ ५१ ॥
चतुःषष्ट्या च मात्रया कुम्भकेनैव धारयेत् ।
तमोमयं शिवं ध्यात्वा मकारं शुक्लवर्णकम् ॥ ५२ ॥
द्वात्रिंशन्मात्रया चैव रेचयेद्विधिना पुनः ।
पुनः पिङ्गलयापूर्य कुम्भकेनैव धारयेत् ॥ ५३ ॥
इडया रेचयेत् पश्चात् तद्बीजेन क्रमेण तु ।
अनुलोमविलोमेन वारंवारं च साधयेत् ॥ ५४ ॥
पूरकान्ते कुम्भकान्तं धृतनासापुटद्वयम् ।
कनिष्ठानामिकाङ्गुष्ठैः तर्जनीमध्यमे विना ॥ ५५ ॥
प्राणायामो निगर्भस्तु विना बीजेन जायते ।
वामजानूपरिन्यस्तवामपाणितलं भ्रमेत् ॥ ५६ ॥
एकादिशतपर्यन्तं पूरकुम्भकरेचनम् ।
उत्तमा विंशतिर्मात्रा षोडशी मात्रा मध्यमा ॥ ५७ ॥
अधमा द्वादशी मात्रा प्राणायामास्त्रिधा स्मृताः ।
अधमाज्जायते घर्मो मेरुकम्पश्च मध्यमात् ॥ ५८ ॥
उत्तमाच्च भूमित्यागस्त्रिविधं सिद्धिलक्षणम् ।
प्राणायामात् खेचरत्वं प्राणायामाद् रोगनाशनम् ॥५९॥
प्राणायामाद्बोधयेच्छक्तिं प्राणायामान्मनोन्मनी ।
आनन्दो जायते चित्ते प्राणायामी सुखी भवेत् ॥६०॥

अथ सूर्यभेदकुम्भकः।

घेरण्ड उवाच—

कथितं सहितं कुम्भं सूर्यभेदनकं शृणु।
पूरयेत् सूर्यनाड्या च यथाशक्ति बहिर्मरुत् ॥ ६१ ॥
धारयेद्बहुयत्नेन कुम्भकेन जलन्धरैः।
यावत् स्वेदं नखकेशाभ्यां तावत् कुर्वन्तु कुम्भकम् ॥ ६२ ॥
प्राणोऽपानः समानश्चोदानव्यानौ तथैव च।
नागः कूर्मश्च कृकरो देवदत्तो धनञ्जयः ॥ ६३ ॥
हृदि प्राणो वहेन्नित्यमपानो गुदमण्डले।
समानो नाभिदेशे तु उदानः कण्ठमध्यगः ॥ ६४ ॥
व्यानो व्याप्य शरीरे तु प्रधानाः पञ्च वायवः।
प्राणाद्याः पञ्च विख्याता नागाद्याः पञ्च वायवः ॥ ६५ ॥
तेषामपि च पञ्चानां स्थानानि च वदाम्यहम्।
उद्गारे नाग आख्यातः कूर्मस्तून्मीलने स्मृतः ॥ ६६ ॥
कृकरः क्षुत्कृते ज्ञेयो देवदत्तो विजृम्भणे।
न जहाति मृते क्वापि सर्वव्यापी धनञ्जयः ॥ ६७ ॥
नागो गृह्णाति चैतन्यं कूर्मश्चैव निमेषणम्।
क्षुत्तृषं कृकरश्चैव जृम्भणं चतुर्थेन तु।
भवेद्धनञ्जयाच्छब्दं क्षणमात्रं न निःसरेत् ॥ ६८ ॥
सर्वे ते सूर्यसंभिन्ना नाभिमूलात् समुद्धरेत्।
ईडया रेचयेत् पश्चात् धैर्येणाखण्डवेगतः ॥ ६९ ॥
पुनः सूर्येण चाकृष्य कुम्भयित्वा यथाविधि।
रेचयित्वा साधयेत्तु क्रमेण च पुनःपुनः ॥ ७० ॥

कुम्भकः सूर्यभेदस्तु जरामृत्युविनाशकः ।
बोधयेत् कुंडलीं शक्तिं देहानलं विवर्धयेत् ।
इति ते कथितं चण्ड सूर्यभेदनमुत्तमम् ॥ ७१ ॥

अथ उज्जायीकुम्भकः ।

नासाभ्यां वायुमाकृष्य मुखमध्ये च धारयेत् ।
हृद्गलाभ्यां समाकृष्य वायुं वक्त्रे च धारयेत् ॥७२॥
मुखं प्रक्षाल्य[1] संवन्द्य[2] कुर्याज्जालन्धरं ततः ।
आशक्ति कुम्भकं कृत्वा धारयेदविरोधतः ॥ ७३ ॥
उज्जायीकुम्भकं[3] कृत्वा सर्वकार्याणि साधयेत् ।
न भवेत् कफरोगश्च क्रूरवायुरजीर्णकम् ॥ ७४ ॥
आमवातः क्षयः कासो ज्वरप्लीहा न विद्यते[4] ।
जरामृत्युविनाशाय चोज्जायीं[5] साधयेन्नरः ॥ ७५ ॥

अथ शीतलीकुम्भकः ।

जिह्वया वायुमाकृष्य उदरे पूरयेच्छनैः ।
क्षणं च कुम्भकं कृत्वा नासाभ्यां रेचयेत् पुनः ॥७६॥
सर्वदा साधयेद्योगी शीतलीकुम्भकं शुभम् ।
अजीर्णं कफपित्तञ्च नैव तस्य प्रजायते ॥ ७७ ॥

अथ भस्त्रिकाकुम्भकः ।

भस्त्रैव लोहकाराणां यथाक्रमेण संभ्रमेत् ।
तथा वायुं च नासाभ्यामुभाभ्यां चालयेच्छनैः॥ ७८ ॥

---

१ प्रफुल्य. २ संबध्य. ३ उज्झायी. ४ जायते. ५ चोज्झायी.

एवं विंशतिवारं च कृत्वा कुर्याच्च कुम्भकम्।
तदन्ते चालयेद्वायुं पूर्वोक्तं च यथाविधि ॥ ७९ ॥
त्रिवारं साधयेदेनं भस्त्रिकाकुम्भकं सुधीः[1]।
न च रोगो न च क्लेश आरोग्यं च दिने दिने ॥८०॥

अथ भ्रामरीकुम्भकः।

अर्धरात्रे गते योगी जन्तूनां शब्दवर्जिते।
कर्णौ पिधाय हस्ताभ्यां कुर्यात् पूरककुम्भकम् ॥८१॥
शृणुयाद्दक्षिणे कर्णे नादमन्तर्गतं शुभम्।
प्रथमं झिञ्झी[2]नादं च वंशीनादं ततः परम् ॥ ८२ ॥
मेघझर्झरभ्रमरीघण्टाकांस्यं ततः परम्।
तुरीभेरीमृदङ्गादिनिनादानकदुन्दुभिः।
एवं नानाविधो नादो जायते नित्यमभ्यसात् ॥ ८३ ॥
अनाहतस्य शब्दस्य तस्य शब्दस्य यो ध्वनिः।
ध्वनेरन्तर्गतं ज्योतिर्ज्योतिरन्तर्गतं मनः ॥ ८४ ॥
तन्मनो विलयं याति तद्विष्णोः परमं पदम्।
एवं भ्रामरीसंसिद्धिः समाधिसिद्धिमाप्नुयात् ॥ ८५ ॥

अथ मूर्च्छाकुम्भकः।

सुखेन कुम्भकं कृत्वा मनश्च भ्रुवोरन्तरम्।
संत्यज्य विषयान् सर्वान् मनोमूर्च्छा सुखप्रदा ॥८६॥
आत्मनि मनसो योगादानन्दो जायते ध्रुवम्।

---

१ सुधीः. २ सिंह.

एवं नानाविधानन्दो जायते नित्यमभ्यसात् ।
एवं मभ्यासयोगेन समाधिसिद्धिमाप्नुयात् ॥ ८७ ॥

अथ केवलीकुम्भकः ।

भुजङ्गिन्याः श्वासवशादजपा जायते ननु ।
हंकारेण बहिर्याति सःकारेण विशेत् पुनः ॥ ८८ ॥
षट्शतानि दिवारात्रौ सहस्राण्येकविंशतिः ।
अजपां नाम गायत्रीं जीवो जपति सर्वदा ॥ ८९ ॥
मूलाधारे यथा हंसस्तथा हि हृदि पङ्कजे ।
तथा नासापुटद्वन्द्वे त्रिभिर्हंससमागमः ॥ ९० ॥
षण्णवत्यङ्गुलीमानं शरीरं कर्मरूपकम् ।
देहाद्बहिर्गतो वायुः स्वभावाद् द्वादशाङ्गुलिः ॥ ९१ ॥
गायने षोडशाङ्गुल्यो भोजने विंशतिस्तथा ।
चतुर्विंशाङ्गुलिः पन्थे निद्रायां त्रिंशदङ्गुलिः ॥ ९२ ॥
मैथुने षट्त्रिंशदुक्तं व्यायामे च ततोधिकम् ।
स्वभावेऽस्य गतेर्न्यूने परमायुः प्रवर्धते ॥ ९३ ॥
आयुःक्षयोऽधिके प्रोक्तो मारुते चान्तराद्गते ।
तस्मात् प्राणे स्थिते देहे मरणं नैव जायते ॥ ९४ ॥
वायुना घटसम्बन्धे भवेत् केवलकुम्भकम् ।
यावज्जीवं जपेन्मन्त्रमजपासंख्यकेवलम् ॥ ९५ ॥
अद्यावधि धृतं संख्याविभ्रमं केवलीकृते ।
अत एव हि कर्तव्यः केवलीकुम्भको नरैः ॥ ९६ ॥

---

१ कारणम्.

केवली चाजपासंख्या द्विगुणा च मनोन्मनी ।
नासाभ्यां वायुमाकृष्य केवलं कुम्भकं चरेत् ॥ ९७ ॥
एकादिकचतुःषष्टिं धारयेत् प्रथमे दिने ।
केवलीमष्टधा कुर्याद् यामे यामे दिने दिने ।
अथवा पञ्चधा कुर्याद् यथा तत् कथयामि ते ॥ ९८ ॥
प्रातर्मध्याह्नसायाह्ने मध्ये रात्रिचतुर्थके ।
त्रिसन्ध्यमथवा कुर्यात् सममाने दिने दिने ॥ ९९ ॥
पञ्चवारं दिने वृद्धिर्वारैकं च दिने तथा ।
अजपापरिमाणं च[1] यावत् सिद्धिः प्रजायते ॥ १०० ॥
प्राणायामं केवलीं च तदा वदति योगवित् ।
केवलीकुम्भके सिद्धे किं न सिद्ध्यति भूतले ॥ १०१ ॥

इति श्रीघेरण्डसंहितायां घेरण्डचण्डसंवादे घटस्थयोगप्रकरणे प्राणायामप्रयोगो नाम पञ्चमोपदेशः ।

षष्ठोपदेशः ।

अथ ध्यानयोगः ।

घेरण्ड उवाच—

स्थूलं ज्योतिस्तथा सूक्ष्मं ध्यानस्य त्रिविधं विदुः ।
स्थूलं मूर्तिमयं प्रोक्तं ज्योतिस्तेजोमयं तथा ।
सूक्ष्मं बिन्दुमयं ब्रह्म कुण्डलीपरदेवता[2] ॥ १ ॥

---

१ वा. २ तम्.

अथ स्थूलध्यानम् ।

स्वकायहृदये ध्यायेत् सुधासागरमुत्तमम् ।
तन्मध्ये रत्नद्वीपं तु सुरत्न[1]वालुकामयम् ॥ २ ॥
चतुर्दिक्षु नीपतरुं बहुपुष्पसमन्वितम् ।
नीपोपवनसंकुलैर्वेष्टितं परिखा इव ॥ ३ ॥
मालतीमल्लिकाजातीकेशरैश्चम्पकैस्तथा ।
पारिजातैः स्थलपद्मैर्गन्धामोदितदिङ्मुखैः ॥ ४ ॥
तन्मध्ये संस्मरेद्योगी कल्पवृक्षं मनोहरम् ।
चतुःशाखाचतुर्वेदं नित्यपुष्पफलान्वितम् ॥ ५ ॥
भ्रमराः कोकिलास्तत्र गुञ्जन्ति निगदन्ति च ।
ध्यायेत्तत्र स्थिरो भूत्वा महामाणिक्यमण्डपम् ॥ ६ ॥
तन्मध्ये तु[2] स्मरेद्योगी पर्यङ्कं सुमनोहरम् ।
तत्रेष्टदेवतां ध्यायेद् यद्ध्यानं गुरुभाषितम् ॥ ७ ॥
यस्य देवस्य यद्रूपं यथा भूषणवाहनम् ।
तद्रूपं ध्यायते नित्यं स्थूलध्यानमिदं विदुः ॥ ८ ॥

प्रकारान्तरम् ।

सहस्रारे महापद्मे कर्णिकायां विचिन्तयेत् ।
विलग्नसहितं[3] पद्मं द्वादशच्छदसंयुतम्[4] ॥ ९ ॥
शुक्लवर्णं महातेजो द्वादशैर्बीजभाषितैम्[5] ।
हसक्षमलवरयुं हसखफ्रें यथाक्रमम्[6] ॥ १० ॥

---

१ वर्ण. २ सं. ३ मङ्कितं. ४ बीजद्वादशसंयुतम्. ५ सहक्ष.
६ मात्.

तन्मध्ये कर्णिकायां तु अकखादि रेखालयम् ।
हलक्षकोणसंयुक्तं प्रणवं तत्र वर्तते ॥ ११ ॥
नादबिंदुमयं पीठं ध्यायेत्तत्र मनोहरम् ।
तत्रोपरि हंसयुग्मं पादुका तत्र वर्तते ॥ १२ ॥
ध्यायेत्तत्र गुरुं देवं द्विभुजं च त्रिलोचनम् ।
श्वेताम्बरधरं देवं शुक्लगन्धानुलेपनम् ॥ १३ ॥
शुक्लपुष्पमयं माल्यं रक्तशक्तिसमन्वितम् ।
एवंविधगुरुध्यानात् स्थूलध्यानं प्रसिध्यति ॥ १४ ॥

अथ ज्योतिध्यानम् ।

घेरण्ड उवाच—

कथितं स्थूलध्यानं तु तेजोध्यानं शृणुष्व मे ।
यद्ध्यानेन योगसिद्धिरात्मप्रत्यक्षमेव च ॥ १५ ॥
मूलाधारे कुण्डलिनी भुजगाकाररूपिणी ।
जीवात्मा तिष्ठति तत्र प्रदीपकलिकाकृतिः ।
ध्यायेत्तेजोमयं ब्रह्म तेजोध्यानं परात्परम् ॥ १६ ॥
नाभिमूले स्थितं सूर्यमण्डलं वन्हिसंयुतम् ।
ध्यायेत्तेजो महद्व्याप्तं तेजोध्यानं तदेव हि ॥ १७ ॥

प्रकारान्तरम् ।

भ्रूमध्ये मनऊर्ध्वे च यत्तेजः प्रणवात्मकम् ।
ध्यायेज्ज्वालावलीयुक्तं तेजोध्यानं तदेव हि ॥ १८ ॥

अथ सूक्ष्मध्यानम् ।

घेरण्ड उवाच—

तेजोध्यानं श्रुतं चण्ड सूक्ष्मध्यानं शृणुष्व मे ।
बहुभाग्यवशाद् यस्य कुण्डली जाग्रती भवेत् ॥ १९ ॥

---

१ था. २ द्वि. ३ तदेव हि.

आत्मना सहयोगेन नेत्ररन्ध्राद्विनिर्गता ।
विहरेद् राजमार्गे च चञ्चलत्वान्न दृश्यते ॥ २० ॥
शाम्भवीमुद्रया योगी ध्यानयोगेन सिध्यति ।
सूक्ष्मध्यानमिदं गोप्यं देवानामपि दुर्लभम् ॥ २१ ॥
स्थूलध्यानाच्छतगुणं तेजोध्यानं प्रचक्षते ।
तेजोध्यानाल्लक्षगुणं सूक्ष्मध्यानं परात्परम् ॥ २२ ॥
इति ते कथितं चण्ड ध्यानयोगं सुदुर्लभम् ।
आत्मा साक्षाद् भवेद् यस्मात्तस्माद्ध्यानं विशिष्यते २३

इति श्रीघेरण्डसंहितायां घेरण्डचण्डसंवादे घटस्थयोगे सप्तमसाधने ध्यानयोगो नाम षष्ठोपदेशः ।

सप्तमोपदेशः ।

अथ समाधियोगः ।

घेरण्ड उवाच—

समाधिश्च परो योगो बहुभाग्येन लभ्यते ।
गुरोः कृपाप्रसादेन प्राप्यते गुरुभक्तितः ॥ १ ॥

विद्याप्रतीतिः स्वगुरुप्रतीति-
रात्मप्रतीतिर्मनसः प्रबोधः ।
दिने दिने यस्य भवेत् स योगी
सुशोभनाभ्यासमुपैति सद्यः ॥ २ ॥

घटाद्भिन्नं मनः कृत्वा ऐक्यं कुर्यात् परात्मनि।
समाधिं तं विजानीयान्मुक्तसंज्ञो[1] दशादिभिः॥ ३॥
अहं ब्रह्म न चान्योऽस्मि ब्रह्मैवाहं न शोकभाक्।
सच्चिदानन्दरूपोऽहं नित्यमुक्तः स्वभाववान्॥ ४॥
शाम्भव्या चैव खेचर्या भ्रामर्या योनिमुद्रया।
ध्यानं नादं रसानन्दं लयसिद्धिश्चतुर्विधा॥ ५॥
पञ्चधा भक्तियोगेन मनोमूर्च्छा च षड्विधा।
षड्विधोऽयं राजयोगः प्रत्येकमवधारयेत्॥ ६॥

अथ ध्यानयोगसमाधिः।

शाम्भवीं मुद्रिकां कृत्वा आत्मप्रत्यक्षमानयेत्।
बिन्दुब्रह्ममयं दृष्ट्वा मनस्तत्र नियोजयेत्॥ ७॥
खमध्ये कुरु चात्मानं आत्ममध्ये च खं कुरु।
आत्मानं खमयं दृष्ट्वा न किञ्चिदपि बुध्यते[2]।
सदानन्दमयो भूत्वा समाधिस्थो भवेन्नरः॥ ८॥

अथ नादयोगसमाधिः।

अनिलं मन्दवेगेन भ्रामरीकुम्भकं चरेत्।
मन्दं मन्दं रेचयेद्वायुं भृङ्गनादं ततो भवेत्॥ ९॥
अन्तःस्थं भ्रमरीनादं श्रुत्वा तत्र मनो नयेत्।
समाधिर्जायते तत्र आनन्दः सोऽहमित्यतः॥ १०॥
खेचरीमुद्रासाधनाद् रसनोर्ध्वगता यदा।
तदा समाधिसिद्धिः स्याद्धित्वा साधारणक्रियाम्॥ ११॥

---

१ गं. २ भावयेत्.

अथ रसानन्दयोगसमाधिः।

योनिमुद्रां समासाद्य[1] स्वयं शक्तिमयो भवेत्।
सुशृङ्गाररसेनैव विहरेत् परमात्मनि ॥ १२ ॥

अथ लयसिद्धियोगसमाधिः।

आनन्दमयः संभूत्वा ऐक्यं ब्रह्मणि सम्भवेत्।
अहं ब्रह्मेति चाद्वैतं समाधिस्तेन जायते ॥ १३ ॥

अथ भक्तियोगसमाधिः।

स्वकीयहृदये ध्यायेदिष्टदेवस्वरूपकम्।
चिन्तयेद् भक्तियोगेन परमाह्लादपूर्वकम् ॥ १४ ॥
आनन्दाश्रुपुलकेन दशाभावः प्रजायते।
समाधिः सम्भवेत्तेन सम्भवेच्च मनोन्मनी ॥ १५ ॥

अथ राजयोगसमाधिः।

मनोमूर्च्छां समासाद्य[2] मन आत्मनि योजयेत्।
परात्मनः समायोगात् समाधिं समवाप्नुयात् ॥ १६ ॥

अथ समाधियोगमाहात्म्यम्।

इति ते कथितश्चण्ड समाधिर्मुक्तिलक्षणम्।
राजयोगसमाधिः स्यादेकात्मन्येव[3] साधनम् ॥ १७ ॥
उन्मनी सहजावस्था सर्वे चैकात्मवाचकाः।
जले विष्णुः स्थले विष्णुर्विष्णुः पर्वतमस्तके ॥ १८ ॥
ज्वालामालाकुले विष्णुः सर्वं विष्णुमयं जगत्।
भूचराः खेचराश्चामी यावन्तो जीवजन्तवः ॥ १९ ॥

---

१ ध्य. २ ध्य. ३ न्ते साक्ष्य.

वृक्षगुल्मलतावल्लीतृणाद्या वारि पर्वताः ।
सर्वं ब्रह्म विजानीयात् सर्वं पश्यति चात्मनि ॥ २० ॥
आत्मा घटस्थचैतन्यमद्वैतं शाश्वतं परम् ।
घटाद्विभिन्नतो[1] ज्ञात्वा वीतरागं विवासनम् ।
एवं मिथः समाधिः स्यात् सर्वसङ्कल्पवर्जितः ॥ २१ ॥
स्वदेहे पुत्रदारादिबान्धवेषु धनादिषु ।
सर्वेषु निर्ममो भूत्वा समाधिं समवाप्नुयात् ॥ २२ ॥
तत्त्वं लयामृतं गोप्यं शिवोक्तं विविधानि च ।
तेषां संक्षेपमादाय कथितं मुक्तिलक्षणम् ॥ २३ ॥
इति ते कथितश्चण्ड समाधिर्दुर्लभः परः ।
यं ज्ञात्वा न पुनर्जन्म जायते भूमिमण्डले ॥ २४ ॥

इति श्रीघेरण्डसंहितायां घेरण्डचण्डसंवादे घटस्थयोगसाधने योगस्य सप्तसारे समाधियोगो नाम सप्तमोपदेशः समाप्तः ।

समाप्त.

---

1 द्भिन्नतरं.

अस्मदीयसंग्रहालये क्रय्यपुस्तकानि.

		डांकव्ययसहितं मूल्यम्.	रु०	आ०
१	ऋग्वेदसंहिता—सायनभाष्यसमेता	....	९०	०
२	ऋग्वेदसंहिता—मूलम्	....	४	८
३	ऋग्वेदीयैतरेयब्राह्मणम्	....	२	१२
४	कृष्णयजुर्वेदसंहिता—मूलम्	....	३	८
५	निरुक्तादिवेदषडङ्गी	....	२	२
६	हठयोगप्रदीपिका—आङ्गलभाषान्तरसहिता.	....	१	८
७	योगसारसंग्रहः	....	०	१०
८	महिम्नः स्तोत्रम्	....	०	२
९	आश्वलायनगृह्यसूत्रं—गार्ग्यनारायणीयवृत्तिसमेतं परिशिष्टसहितं श्रीकुमारिलभट्टस्वामिप्रणीतकारिकाभिः समलंकृतम्.		मुद्राप्यते.	
१०	उपनिषदां अष्टोत्तरशतम्	....	मुद्राप्यते.	

☞ एतानि पुस्तकानि मुम्बापुर्यां यमवाणमिते गृहे (५२)कष्टमहोस रस्तासंज्ञे तुकारामतात्यातः प्राप्नुवन्ति ।

तुकाराम तात्या.